Homemade To Go

The complete guide to co-op cooking

Dee Sarton Bower
&
Mary Eileen Wells

Purrfect Publishing Ltd., Meridian, Idaho

Copyright © 1997
First Printing 1997
Printed in the United States of America

All rights reserved. Photocopies may be made of flyers and forms found in the appendix by the owner of this book for the owner's personal use only. No other part of this book may be reproduced or transmitted in any form or by any means, electronic or mechanical, including photocopying, recording or by any information storage and retrieval system without written permission from the authors, except for inclusion of brief quotations in a review.

Purrfect Publishing Ltd.
Post Office Box 1013
Meridian, ID 83680-1013 U.S.A.

Credits
Front cover picture "Neighborhood Potluck" is by noted artist of Americana,
    Jane Wooster Scott.
Selected illustrations are from *Old-Fashioned Eating and Drinking Illustrations*
    copyright © 1988 by Dover Publications, Inc., and used with permission.
Scripture quotation marked (TEV) is from The Good News Bible, Today's
    English Version — Second Edition copyright © 1992.

Library of Congress Cataloging-in-Publication Data
Bower, Dee Sarton.
     Homemade to go : the complete guide to co-op cooking / Dee Sarton
  Bower and Mary Eileen Wells.
          p.   cm.
     Includes index.
     ISBN 0-9657913-9-4 : $14.95
     1. Cookery. 2. Quantity Cookery. 3. Neighborhood, Community life.
     I. Wells, Mary Eileen. II: Title.
TX820.B69 1997
641.55   97-91843
                                                                                      CIP

"Provision for others is a fundamental responsibility of human life."
—WOODROW WILSON

Table of Contents

Chapter 1 Co-op Cooking – Is it for you? 1
Have your eating habits gone to the dogs? • What is a cooking co–op? • How it all got started • Top ten reasons to start a cooking co–op • Disadvantages of co-op cooking • But I'm not a cook! • Be healthy — have friends

Chapter 2 Forming Your Co-op 5
Determine your own needs • Co-op cooking is versatile • Decide where to find co–op members • Choose the type of co–op you want • Get the word out • Tips for a great first meeting • Call a meeting • Co-op Cooking Start-Up Questionnaire

Chapter 3 Getting Started 11
Frequently asked questions • Family mealtimes earn an A+ • Early American meals to go • Food to keep on hand • Top ten ways to build a successful co-op • Notes about my co-op

Chapter 4 Cooking for a Crowd 19
Multiplying recipes • Rules for multiplying ingredients in recipes • Recipe computer programs • Handy cooking equipment to own • Equivalents • Using Recipe Conversion Cards • How much food to prepare • Substitutes and Equivalents • Tips to make cooking easier • Take it easy

Chapter 5 Food Safety - Or, how <u>not</u> to make your neighbors sick! 27
Rules for cooking safely • Keep your kitchen clean and safe • How to avoid food poisoning "bugs" • Keep hot food hot • Cooking meat and poultry • Keep cold food cold • Be an alert shopper • Take allergies seriously • For more information...

Chapter 6 Planning Your Meals 33
Nutrition first • Make it appetizing! • Use planning calendars • The "kid factor" • Menu ideas

Chapter 7 Recipes 39
Main dishes • Soups • Side dishes • Salads • Desserts

Appendix Things To Make Your Life Easier 63
Flyers • Start-Up Questionnaires • Planning Calendars • Evaluation Sheets • Shopping lists • Recipe Conversion Cards • Dinner Tags

General Index 115

Recipe Index 117

Dedication

This book is dedicated to our husbands, Rick and Terry, and to our children (Sarah, Evan, Emily, Brianne and Chase). Our dinners together are wonderful memories in the making.

Acknowledgments

Special thanks to the following people for their contributions in the development of *Homemade To Go*:

Our fellow co-op families...
    David, Juanita, Nick, Tyler, and Mia Russell, and
    Tom, Kathy, Heather, and Luke Holloway, and their babysitter, Lisa Smeade

Our editors, proof readers, and others with helpful advice...
    Paul Fugleberg, Gayle O'Donahue, Nancy Rush, Marian Cole,
    Daniel and Gwen Sarton, and Kelly Branson

Those who offered their food preparation and nutritional expertise...
    The Central District Health nutrition staff (for reviewing Chapters 4 & 5),
    and Marilyn Cross Bischoff, Extension Educator, University of Idaho
        Cooperative Extension System, Ada County

Our friends and family members who shared their recipes with us...
    Juanita Russell, Kathy Holloway, Marian Cole, Nancy Cooley,
    Lydia Ruppert, Billie Rudzinski, and Kassie Jones

Those who graciously allowed us to use their writings...
    Sue Browder and Carla Milne

And our sponsor Ore-Ida and especially Grant Jones who supported the project
    from the beginning.

Foreword

Does the age-old question, "What's for dinner?" ring through your household every evening? Does putting dinner on the table for your family seem to become a bigger chore? How do you spell relief for these dilemmas? C·O·O·P C·O·O·K·I·N·G. That's right, co-op cooking.

Today, we are all looking to simplify—and economize—our lives. We want to recapture the tradition of gathering family around the dinner table for good food and lively conversation. We are seeking convenience, without sacrificing quality and taste.

Living more simply and economically while providing value is a dream of everyone. Co-op cooking can make the dream come true for you.

Co-op cooking and Ore-Ida products provide a winning recipe for success with your family and neighbors. While the notion of co-op cooking hasn't been around very long, Ore-Ida's tried and true products have been gracing dinner tables across America for over 40 years.

Co-op cooking mirrors Ore-Ida's philosophy: restore the family dinner hour, and help families enjoy economical, timesaving and nutritious meals. Re-emphasizing the neighborhood isn't a bad idea, either!

Enjoy the many mouth-watering recipes in this book. Take advantage of the Ore-Ida coupons for savings on great food for your family and neighbors. You may miss the ring of "What's for dinner?" for a little while, but probably not for long! Happy cooking—and eating!

Grant Jones
Manager, Public Relations
Ore-Ida Foods

For more information about Ore-Ida products, contact Grant Jones at 208/383-6410, gjones@oreida.com, or P.O. Box 10, Boise, ID 83707-0010.

About the authors...

Dee Sarton Bower is a television news anchor, host of Exploring Idaho (seen nationally on The Outdoor Channel), wife and mother of two children. She is also a frequent workshop presenter for business, government, and Christian organizations throughout the Northwest. Dee loves co-op cooking because it gives her more time to enjoy the outdoors with her family, and to play the piano. Dee and her family live outside of Boise, Idaho.

Photography by Stan Sinclair © 1997

Mary Eileen Wells is CEO of Purrfect Publishing Ltd., a former reseacher for The World Bank, a wife and mother of three children. She has taught college level computer science and is now using those skills in the publishing field. Her master's degree in horticulture and training as a master gardener come in handy now that she has more time (thanks to co-op cooking) to spend gardening at her southwest Idaho home.

Photography by Stan Sinclair © 1997

A note to our readers...

While reading this book, which has two authors, you may wonder why it is written from the viewpoint of one person. We found this the best way to solve the problem of identifying the speaker. Rather than constantly using "I, Dee Bower..." or "I, Mary Wells...", we decided it would be easier and less confusing to the reader to use the pronoun "I" throughout the body of the book.

Preface

Twenty years ago I was a Peace Corps volunteer in the West African country, Upper Volta (since renamed Burkina Faso). Buying food involved going to several different vendors in an open market. I would bargain with the "Tomato Lady" for tomatoes, onions and garlic. Eggs, bananas, and other fruit were sold by a prosperous man in a large area in the middle of the market. Dozens of vultures perched on the roofs of stalls where butchers sold meat. At each stop it was customary to shake hands with the merchant and inquire about his or her health and family. Only after these greetings, which could last several minutes, was it considered polite to continue with the business of buying food.

After two years I returned home. It surprises people when I tell them I suffered more from culture shock after my return home than I did when I went to Africa. Interestingly, it was greatest during my first return visit to a local grocery store. No one would look me in the eye. Not one other customer said hello. When I went through the checkout stand the cashier was very efficient, but not once did she smile or inquire about how I was doing. I felt very alone even though I was among a crowd of people, something I never felt in my two years as a Peace Corps volunteer.

I'm not saying life in Upper Volta was perfect. There was poverty, few people could read or write, and I watched the pain in the eyes of more than one woman whose baby or child died from a disease easily prevented by modern medicine and clean drinking water. In America, we enjoy a standard of living far higher than most of us realize. Lights go on with a flick of a switch, there are vaccines to protect our children from the deadly diseases that used to take so many young lives, and we have indoor flush toilets and abundant toilet paper. But we have lost something in our never-ending quest to make life easier, faster, and more hygienic. Families are scattered across the country. On hot summer days we stay in air conditioned homes watching TV instead of sitting on porches visiting neighbors. Many people don't even know their neighbors.

I was feeling lonely one day when my neighbor, Dee Bower, came up with the idea of starting a cooking co-op. Now, after three years of sharing meals with Dee's, Juanita's and Kathy's families, I no longer feel isolated. We trade recipes and stories, borrow aluminum foil and eggs from each other and, most important, our children have other adults who care about them. Dee and I feel so strongly that cooking co-ops can help other people, that we decided to write *Homemade To Go*. In it we share our knowledge and experience in every aspect of starting and maintaining a cooking co-op. We hope you find it useful and informative. *Bon appétit!*

— *Mary Wells*

God bless these friends with whom we eat
God bless the stranger in his seat
God bless the hands this food prepared
God bless each dish as it is shared
— Carla Milne

Chapter 1

Co-op Cooking — Is it for you?

Have your eating habits "gone to the dogs?"

At our house, dinner planning and preparation had become a dreaded daily chore. We had to eat, of course, but I didn't have time to plan, shop, and prepare meals in between work, dance lessons, committee meetings, laundry, church, soccer games, school, dirty diapers, piano recitals... you know what I mean. The busyness of life sabotaged my good intentions for healthy, enjoyable mealtimes. Expensive fast food too often filled the gap. This was our life before I discovered co-op cooking.

Henry David Thoreau once said, "Our life is frittered away by detail… simplify, simplify." I believe he is right, and that's why I believe in co-op cooking. It's a simple way to make life easier and better.

What is a cooking co-op?

*A **cooking co-op** is a group of people who prepare meals for one another on a rotating basis.* You don't have to eat together. One day a week you prepare enough dinner for everyone in your co-op. The other days you rest and dinner is delivered to you.

Co-ops can take many forms, but ours is a neighborhood co-op. We are four families who cook for each other Monday through Thursday. We each have a designated day to prepare meals for the entire group. Our families are about the same size and we all have young children with similar appetites (no teenage boys to throw off the serving size balance). Since we live in the same neighborhood, delivering meals is as easy as loading up the kids' wagons. We have similar lifestyles (busy) and similar tastes in food.

From our experience these four ingredients make for the most successful cooking co-ops:

- Families with similar appetites
- Similar tastes in food
- A convenient way to deliver food
- Similar lifestyles.

How it all got started

"One day I was sitting in the doctor's office…waiting. I had a million things to do, the doctor was running late, and now my split second timing was off by 15 minutes. Out of frustration I grabbed a magazine and started flipping through the pages when my eyes landed on an article that was about to make my life much easier. It was about co-op cooking. I read the article with utter fascination.

"That night I went home with unbridled enthusiasm only to be met by my very skeptical husband, Terry. 'It will never work,' he said. Most of the time I carefully consider Terry's opinion, but this time I was determined. Right away I called my 'can-do' neighbor, Mary. She also saw the potential for taking the stress and drudgery out of dinner time. Within a half-hour she had a meeting lined up with two other families. We got together, worked through a few details, and decided to give it a try. We have been co-op cooking ever since (more than three years now). And Terry? He's the biggest convert you'll ever hope to meet." —Dee

Notice the word "similar." I use it a lot, but don't mistake similar for identical. There are many ways to make your group compatible without having identical-sized families, lifestyles, or tastes in food. I'll talk more about family size in the next chapter.

Once your co-op gets started, it doesn't take long to realize the many advantages. Some are obvious, but I was surprised to find so many unexpected pluses.

Top ten reasons to start a cooking co-op:

- Menus are set up weeks in advance. How wonderful!

- You save money! Planning ahead means you can take advantage of sales and buying in bulk.

- You spend less time in the grocery store. Shopping for one large meal a week is much easier and less time consuming than shopping for five different meals.

- No more last minute expensive, unhealthy fast food meals.

- Your kitchen gets really messy only once a week.

- Dinner-time stress is gone. Imagine, laughter and smiles at the dinner table!

- You maximize your efforts and minimize the time you expend. Your cooking day can be intense, but your "off" days can be spent on other hobbies, interests, or family time.

- Cooking is fun again because you make one special dinner a week instead of daily routine meals.

- Co-op cooking brings people together. It creates a sense of community.

- You always have an answer for that pesky and predictable question, "Mom, what's for dinner?"

Disadvantages of co-op cooking

Well,...hmmm...gee, I can't really think of any.

However, I will mention some reality checks. First, remember... MURPHY'S LAW LIVES! So it stands to reason that on your cooking day other demands will rear their ugly heads. The key is to plan ahead.

> *"For me the best part of the cooking co-op is no longer wandering around the grocery store at 4 P.M. with that panicky feeling, wondering, 'What in the world am I going to fix for dinner?'"*
> —Mary

Second, there is added pressure. After all, what will the neighbors think if the meat loaf tastes like dog food? Stop worrying. Crowd–pleasing recipes are just a few pages ahead. You may occasionally get a meal that is not your favorite, but that happens even when we cook for ourselves.

Finally, cooking day is intense, especially in the beginning. You will need to set aside several hours (it takes me about three hours of preparation and cooking time) to get the job done. Once in your schedule, cooking day becomes routine, but don't try to fit other responsibilities into your cooking time. Dedicate the necessary hours just to co-op cooking. After all, buying pizza for several families can be expensive.

But I'm not a cook!

That was my biggest concern when I joined the co-op. I didn't enjoy cooking and I wasn't very good at it. But, I didn't let that stop me. I set out to find easy to prepare recipes that wouldn't overwhelm me. I've included our favorites in Chapter 7. The ability to follow directions, common sense and a little courage are all you need. Two or three weeks into co-op cooking and you'll wonder what you ever worried about.

Be healthy — have friends

Having a network of supportive family and friends has been linked to fewer complications in pregnancy (and shorter labor during delivery), higher levels of immune function, and a greater ability to give up cigarettes, stick with an exercise program and even survive cancer...

In one study in Alameda County, California, adults who had the fewest connections with other people were the most likely to die of heart disease, cerebrovascular disease, cancer and other illnesses.

—SUE BROWDER
EXCERPTED WITH PERMISSION FROM THE SEPTEMBER 1996 READER'S DIGEST

"The best way to clean a frying pan that has burned food cemented to the bottom is to let it soak in soapy water for several days and then, when nobody is looking, throw it in the garbage."

—DAVE BARRY, THE MIAMI HERALD

Chapter 2

Forming Your Co-op

Now that you know all the advantages of co-op cooking, it's time to jump in with both feet! This chapter will help you assess your own needs, choose the type of co-op that best suits you, and help you find the perfect people to join your co-op.

Step 1 - Determine your own needs

It's a good idea to figure out your own needs before you start a cooking co-op. Indicate your dietary needs and preferences, and how much your family eats below:

Dietary needs and preferences

____ Meat and potatoes only
____ Reasonable and varied diet
____ Low fat / low cholesterol
____ Vegetarian
____ Kosher
____ Food allergies _____
____ Other (specify) _____

Family appetite

____ Total servings you normally prepare. (Think in terms of how much your family eats rather than how many mouths there are to feed. A family with two adults and three small children may eat about the same for dinner as a family with one adult and two teenagers. Since they require the same amount of food these two families would be compatible co-op members.)

Keep in mind your family's appetite and dietary needs and preferences as you begin your search for other co-op members. They are the first two elements of a successful cooking co-op as discussed in Chapter 1:

- Families with similar appetites
- Similar tastes in food
- A convenient way to deliver food
- Similar lifestyles

Co-op cooking is versatile

"About a year after we'd started our co-op, I got a call from an acquaintance in a small town nearby. She had heard about our group and wanted more information. Her husband is pastor of a church and they thought forming cooking co-ops would be a creative way to encourage fellowship within their congregation (not to mention offer their members a wonderful time saving tool). Her idea was to invite the congregation to a meeting and then help them divide into groups according to their dietary needs. There seemed to be some natural groupings. For example, there were a number of families just starting low-fat diets, many of the widows had lost interest in cooking now that they were alone, and young mothers were having a hard time juggling work, children, and mealtime. Because it's a small town, delivering food wouldn't be a problem, but she also thought some families might want to swap frozen meals on Sunday mornings. This was a very exciting development. It made us realize just how versatile co-op cooking can be. You can make your co-op anything you want it to be." —Dee

Step 2 - Decide where to find co-op members

Where can you find people who will benefit from co-op cooking as much as you will? Your neighborhood is a good place to start. Meal delivery and exchange of food containers is easy and convenient, and you and your neighbors are likely to have similar lifestyles (the third and fourth elements of a successful cooking co-op). You have the added benefit of getting to know your neighbors better. If your neighborhood doesn't seem like a possibility, consider these options:

- Work — Work is a convenient place to exchange meals (as long as the boss doesn't mind). You'll need a place to keep your food cold, of course. A refrigerator or plug-in cooler is all you need to make a work swap possible.

- Church (or synagogue) — Here is a natural place to connect with others who might like to form a co-op. What a wonderful way to grow closer to your church family.

- Support and special interest groups — If you belong to a support group, consider exploring the co-op idea with them. Single moms and dads, people on special diets (to lose weight or to deal with health problems), senior citizens — the possibilities are endless. Just about any group that gets together frequently could be your source for co-op members.

Step 3 - Choose the type of co-op you want

As you consider who might join your co-op, think about the best way to share your meals. There are basically two approaches: fresh or frozen. If you exchange your meals with people you see frequently, such as neighbors or coworkers, fresh daily is a great option and will give you the greatest benefits. Aside from just heating up your dinner and maybe cooking spaghetti or noodles, your dinner is ready to eat. You will appreciate this fact when you and your family come home hungry and dinner is ready in just minutes. This book deals primarily with this type of co-op.

If you form a co-op with people you see less frequently, then freezing your meals will work best. This option has two major drawbacks. You are limited in the types of dishes that you can prepare, and you have to take time to thaw your meals.

Step 4 - Get the word out

Now that you know your target group, you'll want to get people interested in joining your co-op. This book can be a great tool for sparking interest. Show

Tips for a great first meeting

Friendly open discussion will get off to a good start if you make everyone feel at home and pay attention to these details:

1) make introductions,
2) serve simple refreshments,
3) arrange chairs in a circle,
4) have extra paper and pencils.

it to your friends and neighbors and see what happens. We've also included flyers that you can distribute or post to advertise your co-op.

Step 5 - Call a meeting

It's time to call a meeting once you have enough interested people to get started. Your goal is to explain co-op cooking in detail (be sure to read Chapter 3: Getting Started) and find out if everyone is compatible. That's where the Co-op Cooking Start-Up Questionnaire comes in handy. It's your most important tool in forming a successful co-op. Everyone needs to answer the questions honestly and discuss them thoroughly. A copy of the questionnaire appears at the end of this chapter and in the appendix.

After discussing the questionnaire you will have one more question left to answer: SHALL WE FORM A CO-OP? If the answer is *yes*, congratulations! You're on your way to a fun and rewarding new outlook on meals and sharing.

Turn the page and use Chapter 3 as a guide to develop a co-op that best meets your needs.

Advertise your co-op

Distribute or post flyers to help advertise your co-op. Full-sized flyers can be found in the appendix.

Co-op Cooking Start-Up Questionnaire

Name: _____ Phone: _____
Address: _____

1. What kind of meals do you prefer?
   - ☐ Fresh meals made daily.
   - ☐ Frozen meals exchanged weekly or monthly.
   - ☐ It doesn't matter to me.

2. What do you want your meals to consist of?
   - ☐ A complete, balanced meal that includes a meat or meat substitute, a side dish of salad, vegetables or fruit, and a carbohydrate such as bread, pasta, rice or potato.
   - ☐ Main dish only.
   - ☐ It doesn't matter to me.

3. Where do you prefer to make the meal exchange?
   - ☐ Neighborhood
   - ☐ Church
   - ☐ Work
   - ☐ Other _____

4. What are your family's dietary needs and preferences? (Check all that apply)
   - ☐ Meat and potatoes only
   - ☐ Reasonable and varied diet
   - ☐ Low fat / low cholesterol
   - ☐ Vegetarian
   - ☐ Kosher
   - ☐ Food allergies (specify) _____
   - ☐ Other (specify) _____

5. What is your family size?
   - ☐ Single
   - ☐ Couple
   - ☐ ____ Adults (including teenagers) and ____ young children

6. How many servings do you usually cook for your family? _____

7. Are there any foods that your family will not eat? _____

8. What is your family's all-time favorite meal? _____

9. Which day of the week would be most convenient for you to cook? _____

10. What is the earliest time of day you are likely to eat dinner? _____

11. I agree to read the chapter on food safety in *Homemade To Go* by Bower and Wells, and to follow the recommendations given. (yes / no)

Notes:

Home is the only place where you can really enjoy fried chicken, corn-on-the-cob and soup!

Chapter 3

Getting Started

With your co-op raring to go there are some details to work out. How does a cooking co-op work? What type of dishes do you use? How do you deliver meals? Read this chapter for the answers to these and other commonly asked questions about co-op cooking. Jot down notes about your co-op on page 17.

Frequently asked questions

How does a cooking co-op work?
A cooking co-op is a group of people who prepare meals for one another on a rotating basis. One day a week you prepare enough dinner for everyone in your co-op. The other days you rest while someone else does the cooking.

Do you eat together?
No. Occasionally, for the fun of it, we'll have a meal together but co-op cooking is not communal cooking. We enjoy seeing each other briefly during the food exchange, but mealtime remains a family affair.

What do you fix, a complete meal or just the main dish?
That's entirely up to your group. Some co-ops share only the main dish, others prepare a full course meal. Our co-op prepares the main dish, one side dish, and often some type of bread. Once in a while we treat each other to dessert. Your co-op can be as simple or complex as you want.

How do you make sure you don't have chicken four nights in a row?
Get together with your co-op members to prepare a menu calendar. (We do this every six weeks.) You'll find a blank calendar in the appendix to use. Everyone should come to the meeting with menu ideas. Plug the menus into the calendar with variety in mind. Have someone in the group make copies of the calendar for all co-op families.

How much time does it take to prepare dinner on your cooking day?
Generally three to four hours. The preparation time can vary greatly, however, depending on the menu you've chosen. It's a good idea to plan your menus according to the time you have to spend. Keep side dishes simple if your main dish is time consuming and vice versa.

Is dinner delivered hot and ready to eat?
Sometimes, but most often the meal needs to be warmed, or some minor preparation may be needed. For example, pasta is usually delivered uncooked so it won't be sticky.

"The comment I hear most often goes something like this: 'I don't think I'd like that many people eating at my house every week.' I wouldn't either. That's why we <u>deliver</u> the food to each family in our group on our cooking day" —Mary

What kind of containers do you use?

Our co-op bought four identical sets of dishes. Each set consists of two clear oven-safe glass casseroles with plastic lids (an 11-cup rectangular and a 7-cup round). They are versatile and can be used for just about anything from cooking to storing. We usually put the main dish in the large rectangular casserole and the side dish in the round bowl. The size of your dishes will be determined by the size of your families. We highly recommend buying identical dishes for co-op use to prevent favorite dishes from getting lost in the shuffle.

Our co-op also purchased four 2-quart plastic containers with screw top lids. They come in handy for soup, gravy, and sauces (like spaghetti sauce).

We sometimes use plastic bags for green salads or vegetables. Large plastic yogurt containers, baby food jars and clear plastic containers from the deli all come in handy when delivering food. Baby food jars are just the right size for delivering salad dressing. The larger containers can be used for fruit salad, and salsa.

How do you know how much food to fix?

At your first planning meeting get an idea of how much each family eats. Chapter 4 also gives you guidelines for the amount of food to prepare. After cooking for each other for a few weeks, hold a follow-up meeting to get feedback on the amount of food being delivered.

How do you make sure your portions are equally divided?

Most of the time you can eyeball it, but weigh and measure the food if it makes you feel more comfortable. Having identical dishes helps a lot. Simply divide your meals into the appropriate containers.

How do you deliver the meals?

If you're part of a neighborhood co-op, just load up a kid's wagon and go door to door. We're able to fit our dishes into a plastic grocery bag for each family, and they fit nicely into the wagon. If you'll be transporting food in the car, put the meals in a cooler.

When do you deliver the meals?

That's an important decision to make as a group. Question 10 of the Co-op Cooking Start-Up Questionnaire asks "What is the earliest time of day you are likely to eat dinner?" If the earliest time any family eats is five o'clock, set that as the latest time dinner will be ready. If dinner takes longer to cook than you expect (and this has happened to all of us), call and let the other families know.

Family mealtimes earn an A+

Want your kids to do well in school? Keep the family dinner hour sacred and see the results on their report cards.

A recent Reader's Digest Poll revealed a fascinating connection between shared mealtimes and academic success. High school students who eat meals with their families four or more times a week score consistently higher on academic tests.

Experts say shared meals mean shared lives. In our hectic world dinner is time to pause and give the message, "We care about what's going on with you."

Some co-ops don't include delivery at all. Members simply drop by the home of the family that has prepared dinner and pick it up. Again, set a time when it can be picked up.

If you're exchanging meals at a central location (work or church for example) food delivery is simply a matter of deciding on a convenient time and place to pick up your dinner.

How much do you spend on each meal?

This is something each co-op needs to decide for itself. We suggest you start with a tentative budget in mind. Then keep track of how much each family spends the first week. Take the group's average and make that your limit. It is important to have a budget so that you don't feel you have to keep up with the others. Your meals could end up being more and more expensive. We decided to limit our spending to about $35 per meal. That's enough for 20 servings of a meat, vegetable and bread. Sometimes we spend a little more or a little less. In the long run it averages out.

Who washes the dishes?

You do — and be sure to get your clean dishes to the next cook bright and early in the morning. We put our dishes in plastic grocery bags and set them by the front door.

Can families of different sizes join a co-op?

Sure. I know of a co-op that consists of five families — three have four family members each, and two are older couples with no children at home. The larger families each provide one meal a week. The couples share a cooking day so that each one cooks every other week. The couples each receive half the amount of food as the larger families.

Do you ever stop the cooking co-op?

Occasionally we'll suspend the co-op for a week or two. This usually happens around the holidays or during busy vacation times.

What do you do when one of the co-op families goes on vacation?

The vacationing family simply drops out of the co-op for the week. You will have one less family to cook for, and of course you won't get a meal on that family's cooking day. Otherwise everything stays the same.

Early American meals to go

The early Puritans in Boston strictly observed the Sabbath. In order to have a hot meal on Sundays, the local baker would come by on Saturday and pick up their filled bean pots. He would bake the beans and return them on Sunday along with fresh baked loaves of brown bread.

What do you do if you're having company?

If your co-op is in the habit of completing a six-week calendar then you'll know what kind of meal to expect. Think of a few complimentary dishes and serve dinner family-style so everyone can get a little of all the food prepared. The other option is to freeze the co-op meal for later use.

What do you do if an emergency crops up on your cooking day?

If the emergency is a crisis or sudden illness, forget cooking and let everyone know what's happening. Your co-op members will understand.

If your emergency is less serious in nature (like being called into work early) have a backup plan. For example, I keep Rosetto ravioli in my freezer and spaghetti sauce in the pantry for a quick no fuss meal. I've also had to order pizza for everybody in a pinch. It's a good idea to talk about this kind of situation with your co-op members before it occurs. Find out what kind of meals they would find acceptable. You could also offer to trade days with someone else or cook on a day when no one else is.

How do you make sure there are no "spoon-lickers" in your co-op?

Be sure to talk about sanitary standards at the first organizational meeting. The Co-op Cooking Start-Up Questionnaire in Chapter 2 (and the appendix) provides a way to make everyone aware of the importance of cleanliness and safe food preparation. Question 11 says, "I agree to read the chapter on food safety in *Homemade To Go* by Bower and Wells, and to follow the recommendations given." Go over Chapter 5 as a group and make sure everyone understands the basic rules of cooking safety.

How do you avoid problems between co-op members?

Hopefully you will avoid many problems by talking through potential difficulties ahead of time. That's why we stress the importance of an organizational meeting to get everyone on the same wavelength. Unspoken expectations can derail a co-op, so talk about everything until there is common understanding.

Another tool to keep your co-op on track is the Co-op Cooking Evaluation Sheet. It gives everyone an opportunity to give honest yet sensitive feedback. Use the Co-op Cooking Evaluation Sheet every three to six months. You can find copies of it in the appendix.

Food to keep on hand

It's a good idea to keep foods on hand to complement your co-op meals. For example, one of our co-op families keeps a supply of jellied cranberry sauce for when they receive turkey. Other items you might want to stock up on are:

Jars (or dry mixes) of gravy
Frozen mashed potatoes
Frozen dinner rolls
Canned / frozen vegetables
Dried pasta
Applesauce
Barbecue sauce, salsa, hot mustard, catsup

Top Ten Ways To Build A Successful Co-op

1. Be generous with compliments.

2. Be honest but sensitive when a co-op member asks for feedback on a meal.

3. Expect an occasional flop and be forgiving of mistakes. It happens to all of us, even when we're cooking for ourselves.

4. When you need cooking advice, ask a more experienced co-op member for help. They'll be flattered.

5. Be thoughtful. Deliver containers and meals at times agreed upon. Keep your menu calendar up to date.

6. Keep chit chat friendly and brief when delivering meals. Remember, people are hungry!

7. Surprise your group with a special dessert just to say "thanks."

8. If you notice one of your families has out-of-town guests, provide enough food for everyone — just to be nice. The favor will most certainly be returned.

9. If a co-op member is continually catty about another member's cooking, remind them that problems should be dealt with directly and sensitively. If they can't solve the problem in a private and positive manner, perhaps co-op cooking isn't for them.

10. Remember each other in some simple way during the holidays. Celebrate the wonderful bond that develops by intertwining your lives through co-op cooking.

Notes about my co-op:

Cooking Day   Co-op member

_____   _____

_____   _____

_____   _____

_____   _____

_____   _____

Our meals will provide ____ servings per family and consist of (check all that apply):
  ____ main dish   ____ bread
  ____ side dish   ____ dessert
  ____ salad

Our meal budget is $_____

We ____ deliver / ____ pick up meals. Meals will be ready by _____ o'clock.

Dietary preferences (i.e. low-fat, vegetarian, kosher, etc.):

Foods to avoid (allergies or dislikes):

Acceptable emergency meals are:

Our next meeting is:

Notes:

Let the cook who never errs cast the first meatball.

Chapter 4

Cooking for a Crowd

Nothing will make you feel more productive or time efficient than cooking for a crowd. The extra effort pays off in a big way, and the hints in this chapter will give you the confidence you need to move forward and cook your first co-op meal.

Multiplying recipes

You should see my recipe note cards. When I first started co-op cooking I'd scribble the amounts I needed to multiply ingredients all over the card. That was before I made a big mistake (6 tablespoons salt instead of 3). We developed recipe conversion cards (found in the appendix) to prevent further disasters. I recommend you use them to multiply your own recipes. You'll also notice that we've multiplied the recipes in Chapter 7 for you.

Rules for multiplying ingredients in recipes

Baked Goods - It is usually safe to double recipes for baked goods, but do not multiply by three or more. Breads and cakes depend on chemical reactions to rise.

Seasonings in soups, stews, and other dishes that may lose liquid or cook for a long period of time - Do not multiply across the board or your dish will be too highly seasoned. If you multiply a recipe by four, multiply the amount of seasonings by about three. Taste and add more if necessary. The following are considered seasonings: salt, pepper, herbal salt substitutes, herbs, spices, flavorings and extracts, dehydrated onion flakes, and dry seasoning mixes.

When multiplying <u>seasonings</u> in soups, stews, and similar dishes (see above) *use the chart below. Taste and add more if desired. Examples of seasonings include salt, pepper, herbal salt substitutes, herbs, spices, flavorings and extracts, dehydrated onion flakes, garlic powder, and dry seasoning mixes.*

Original Amount	Multiply by 2	Multiply by 3	Multiply by 4	Multiply by 5	Multiply by 6
dash	dash	⅛ tsp	⅛ tsp	¼ tsp	¼ tsp
⅛ tsp	¼ tsp	¼ tsp	¼ + ⅛ tsp	½ tsp	½ tsp
¼ tsp	¼ + ⅛ tsp	½ tsp	½ + ¼ tsp	1 tsp	1 ⅛ tsp
½ tsp	½ + ¼ tsp	1⅛ tsp	½ Tbsp*	2 tsp	2¼ tsp
1 tsp	½ Tbsp*	2¼ tsp	1 Tbsp	1 Tbsp + a scant tsp	1½ Tbsp*
½ Tbsp*	2¼ tsp	1 Tbsp + a scant ½ tsp	1½ Tbsp*	2 Tbsp	2 Tbsp + a scant tsp
2 tsp	1 Tbsp	1½ Tbsp*	2 Tbsp	2½ Tbsp*	3 Tbsp
1 Tbsp	1½ Tbsp*	2 Tbsp + a scant tsp	3 Tbsp	¼ cup	¼ cup + ½ Tbsp*
2 Tbsp	3 tbsp	¼ cup	¼ cup + 2 Tbsp	½ cup	½ cup + 1 Tbsp
¼ cup	¼ cup + 2 Tbsp	½ cup	¾ cup	1 cup	1 cup + 2 Tbsp

* ½ Tbsp = 1½ tsp

Chapter 4: Cooking for a Crowd - 21

What is NOT a seasoning? Most foods including flour, sugar, milk, fruits and vegetables, fresh onions and garlic, candied citrus peel, condiments and sauces (prepared mustard, soy sauce, barbecue sauce, catsup, salsa, prepared horseradish, and hot pepper sauce).

Multiplying ingredients: *Most ingredients, except for seasonings in soups, stews and similar dishes (see previous page), can be multiplied across the board. Use the table below as a guide.*

Original Amount	Multiply by 2	Multiply by 3	Multiply by 4	Multiply by 5	Multiply by 6
dash	⅛ tsp	⅛ tsp	¼ tsp	¼ tsp	¼ + ⅛ tsp
⅛ tsp	¼ tsp	¼ + ⅛ tsp	½ tsp	½ + ⅛ tsp	½ + ¼ tsp
¼ tsp	½ tsp	½ + ¼ tsp	1 tsp	1¼ tsp	½ Tbsp*
½ tsp	1 tsp	½ Tbsp*	2 tsp	2½ tsp	1 Tbsp
1 tsp	2 tsp	1 Tbsp	1 Tbsp + 1 tsp	1 Tbsp + 2 tsp	2 Tbsp
½ Tbsp*	1 Tbsp	1½ Tbsp*	2 Tbsp	2½ Tbsp*	3 Tbsp
2 tsp	1 Tbsp + 1 tsp	2 Tbsp	2 Tbsp + 2 tsp	3 Tbsp + 1 tsp	¼ cup
1 Tbsp	2 Tbsp	3 Tbsp	¼ cup	¼ cup + 1 Tbsp	¼ cup + 2 Tbsp
¼ cup	½ cup	¾ cup	1 cup	1¼ cups	1½ cups
⅓ cup	⅔ cup	1 cup	1⅓ cups	1⅔ cups	2 cups (1 pint)
½ cup	1 cup	1½ cups	2 cups (1 pint)	2½ cups	3 cups
⅔ cup	1⅓ cups	2 cups (1 pint)	2⅔ cups	3⅓ cups	4 cups (1 quart)
¾ cup	1½ cups	2¼ cups	3 cups	3¾ cups	4½ cups
1 cup	2 cups (1 pint)	3 cups	4 cups (1 quart)	5 cups	6 cups (1½ quarts)

Weights

2 oz.	4 oz. (¼ lb.)	6 oz.	8 oz. (½ lb.)	10 oz.	12 oz. (¾ lb.)
4 oz. (¼ lb.)	8 oz. (½ lb.)	12 oz. (¾ lb.)	16 oz. (1 lb.)	20 oz. (1 lb. 4 oz)	24 oz. (1 lb. 8 oz.)
6 oz.	12 oz. (¾ lb.)	18 oz. (1 lb. 2 oz.)	24 oz. (1 lb. 8 oz.)	30 oz. (1 lb. 14 oz.)	36 oz. (2 lb. 4 oz.)
8 oz. (½ lb.)	16 oz. (1 lb.)	24 oz. (1 lb. 8 oz.)	32 oz. (2 lb.)	40 oz. (2 lb. 8 oz.)	48 oz. (3 lb.)
12 oz. (¾ lb.)	24 oz. (1 lb. 8 oz.)	36 oz. (2 lb. 4 oz.)	48 oz. (3 lb.)	60 oz. (3 lb. 12 oz.)	72 oz. (4 lb. 8 oz.)
14 oz.	28 oz. (1 lb. 12 oz.)	42 oz. (2 lb. 10 oz.)	56 oz. (3 lb. 8 oz.)	70 oz. (4 lb. 6 oz.)	84 oz. (5 lb. 4 oz.)
16 oz. (1 lb.)	32 oz. (2 lb.)	48 oz. (3 lb.)	64 oz. (4 lb.)	80 oz (5 lb.)	96 oz. (6 lb.)
20 oz. (1 lb. 4 oz)	40 oz. (2 lb. 8 oz.)	60 oz. (3 lb. 12 oz.)	80 oz (5 lb.)	100 oz. (6 lb. 4 oz.)	120 oz. (7 lb. 8 oz.)

* ½ Tbsp = 1½ tsp

Recipe computer programs

If you like to use the computer, cookbook programs can come in handy. Find a program that allows you to enter your own recipes. You can then automatically multiply the recipe for as many servings as you desire and print out a paper copy to use while cooking. Some programs will even compile a shopping list for you based on your menu.

Handy cooking equipment to own

You don't need a lot of fancy equipment to cook for a crowd, but we've found the following items are helpful in addition to your normal pots and pans. You may already own many.

- a stock pot for soups and stews
- a food processor to help with chopping, shredding and slicing
- a large frying pan or wok
- meat thermometer
- measuring cup set that includes ¼, ⅓, ½, ⅔, ¾ and one cup measures
- measuring spoon set that includes ⅛, ¼, ½, one teaspoon, and ½ and one tablespoon measures

Equivalents

3 tsp	= 1 Tbsp
4 Tbsp	= ¼ cup
8 Tbsp	= ½ cup
2 cups	= 1 pint
4 cups	= 1 quart
2 pints	= 1 quart
4 quarts	= 1 gal.
16 oz.	= 1 lb.
1 oz. liquid	= 2 Tbsp
8 oz. liquid	= 1 cup
32 oz. liquid	= 1 quart

Using Recipe Conversion Cards

You'll want to use your favorite recipes when cooking for your co-op families. Cooking will go more smoothly and you'll make fewer mistakes if you have everything written out beforehand. Recipe Conversion Cards are provided for you in the appendix for this purpose. Write out the ingredients and the amounts called for in the original recipe, and then multiply them out in the appropriate blanks. When multiplying <u>seasonings</u> in soups, stews, and other dishes that may lose liquid or cook for a long period of time, use the table on page 20. Follow the table on page 21 when multiplying all other ingredients.

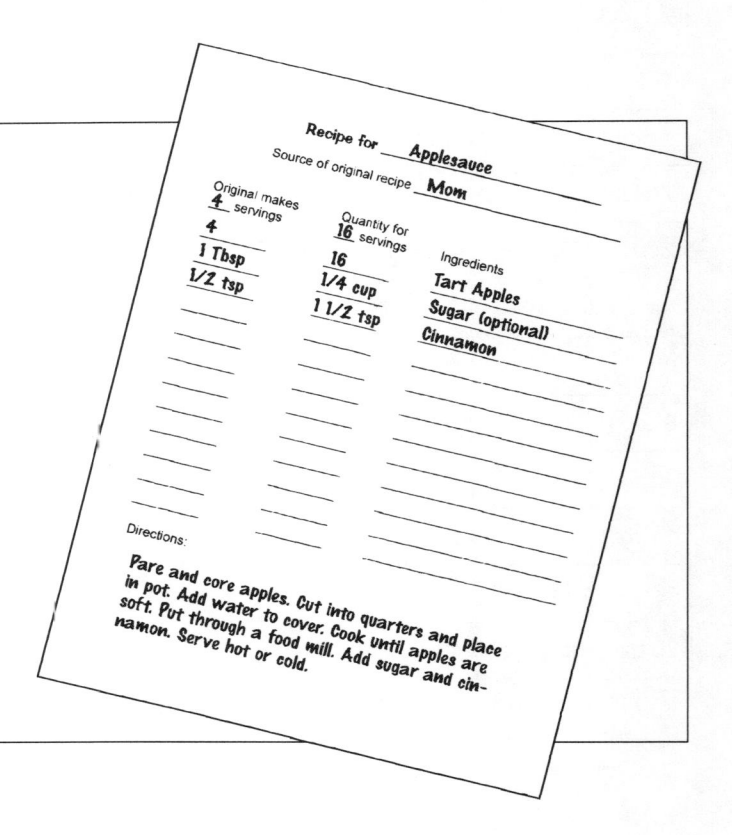

How much food to prepare

Rolls and Bread
Rolls — 2 per person
Bread — One loaf French, Italian or other bread per family (serves up to 10)

Soups and Stews
One to 2 cups per person (leftovers are always appreciated)

Salads and Vegetables
Green leaf salad — one cup per serving
Potato — ½ cup per serving
Fruit — ¾ to one cup per serving
Cooked vegetables — ½ cup per serving

Meat
Boneless (ground beef lamb and veal, boneless stew, boned roasts and steaks, flank, tenderloin, variety meats) — ¼ pound per serving = 4 servings per pound

Some bone (rib roasts, unboned steaks, chops, ham) — ½ pound per serving = 2 servings per pound

Bony cuts (short ribs, spareribs, lamb shanks, shoulder, breast and plate cuts, brisket and hock) —1 pound per serving

Poultry
Roasted turkey breast — ⅓ pound per serving = 3 servings per pound

Whole turkey
  less than 12 pounds — ¾ to 1 pound per serving = 1 to 1⅓ serving per pound
  over 12 pounds — ½ to ¾ pound per serving = 1⅓ to 2 servings per pound

Whole chickens, halves or quarters — ¾ pound per serving = 1⅓ servings per pound

Chicken breasts — one-half breast per serving

Goose or gosling — one pound per serving

Fish
Small, whole fish — one pound per serving
Small fish with head, fins, tail, and entrails removed — ¾ pound per serving
  = 1⅓ servings per pound

Fish fillets — ⅓ pound per serving = 3 servings per pound
Fish steaks — ⅓ pound per serving = 3 servings per pound

Substitutes and Equivalents

Apples	1 lb. unpared	3 cups pared and sliced
Arrowroot (for thickening)	1½ teaspoons	1 tablespoon flour
	2 teaspoons	1 tablespoon cornstarch
Baking powder (for rising)	1 teaspoon	¼ tsp baking soda plus ⅝ tsp cream of tartar
Bread Crumbs, dry	¼ cup	1 slice bread
soft	½ cup	1 slice bread
Cabbage	1 pound (1 head)	4½ cups shredded
Carrots, fresh (no tops)	1 pound	2½ cups diced
Cheese, shredded	¼ pound	1 cup
Chicken, boneless, skinless	1 pound uncooked	about 3 cups cooked and cubed
Chocolate, unsweetened	1 oz.	3 Tbsp. cocoa plus 1 Tbsp butter
	1 oz. plus 4 tsp. sugar	1⅔ ounce semisweet chocolate
Cracker crumbs	¾ cup	1 cup bread crumbs
Cream, whipping	1 cup unwhipped	2 to 2½ cups whipped
Flour (for thickening)	1 tablespoon	1½ teaspoons cornstarch or arrowroot starch
Garlic	1 small clove	⅛ teaspoon powder
Herbs, fresh chopped	1 tablespoon	⅓ teaspoon powdered or ½ teaspoon crushed
Honey	1 cup	1¼ cups sugar plus ¼ cup liquid
Lemon	1	3 tablespoons juice, 1 to 1½ teaspoon grated rind
	1 teaspoon juice	½ teaspoon vinegar
	1 tsp. grated rind	½ teaspoon lemon extract
Macaroni, uncooked	1 pound	4 to 5 cups
Macaroni, 1-inch pieces	1 cup uncooked	2 to 2¼ cups cooked
Marshmallows	1 cup cut up	16 large or 160 miniature
Meat		
Beef, cooked	1 pound	3 cups minced
Beef, uncooked	1 pound	2 cups ground
Milk, whole	1 cup	½ cup evaporated plus ½ cup water, or 1 cup reconstituted nonfat dry milk plus 2½ teaspoons butter or margarine
Milk, skim	1 cup	⅓ cup instant nonfat dry milk plus ¾ cup water
Milk, to sour	1 cup	Add 1 Tbsp lemon juice or vinegar to 1 cup milk minus 1 tablespoon. Let sit for 5 minutes.
Mushrooms, fresh	8 oz. or 3 cups	1 cup sliced, cooked
Mushrooms, canned	6 oz. drained	½ pound fresh
Mustard	1 teaspoon dry	1 tablespoon prepared
Noodles, uncooked	1 pound	6 to 8 cups
Noodles, 1-inch pieces	1 cup uncooked	About 1¼ cups cooked
Orange	1 medium	6 to 8 tablespoons orange
Orange	1 medium	¾ cup cut up
Orange rind, grated	1 medium	2 to 3 tablespoons
Peppers, green	6 oz. or 1 large	1 cup diced
Potatoes	1 lb. sliced or diced	3½ to 4 cups raw
	1 lb. or 3 medium	2¼ cups cooked or 1¾ cups mashed
Rice, uncooked	1 lb. or 2 cups	6 cups cooked (about)
Rice, instant	2 cups	2⅔ cups cooked
Tomatoes	1 cup packed	½ cup tomato sauce plus ½ cup water
Tomato juice	1 cup	½ cup tomato sauce plus ½ cup water
Tomato sauce	2 cups	¾ cup tomato paste plus 1 cup water

Tips to make cooking easier

Tip 1 - Don't try to do too much!
It's usually best to prepare only one difficult dish for each meal. For example, suppose you want to prepare Tangy Vegetable Potato Salad, which takes time to cut up and prepare. Serve it with broiled steak or fish, very easy but popular dishes, and purchased bread. You'll have a great meal and won't wear yourself out.

Tip 2 - Plan ahead
By keeping a calendar (see Chapter 6 and the appendix) you will always know what you'll be cooking and can plan ahead. Shop several days before for nonperishables and for what can be prepared ahead of time. Shop on your cooking day for fresh fruit, vegetables and bread.

Tip 3 - Don't do everything from scratch
There are many products you can use to make your cooking day go more smoothly without sacrificing quality. Examples are frozen bread dough, Ore-Ida Frozen Mashed Potatoes, frozen pie crusts, and frozen vegetables. When deciding what foods to use, weigh your time and energy versus the cost of the product.

Tip 4 - Plan your stir-fry dishes carefully
Stir-fry dishes can be difficult unless planned carefully. Cut up and measure all ingredients before starting. If using raw vegetables, cooking times vary. For instance, it takes longer to cook broccoli than mushrooms. Thus, use a frozen stir-fry vegetable mix (the vegetables are prepared to cook in the same amount of time) and fresh meat. Microwave the vegetables while you stir-fry the meat on the stove. Divide the vegetables between your co-op dishes and top with the meat.

Tip 5 - Deliver salad and dressing separately
Lettuce tends to get soggy if dressing is left on it for any amount of time. For highest quality, put salads in one container, dressing in another and croutons in plastic sandwich bags. Just before serving, your co-op families can toss all ingredients together in a bowl.

Tip 6 - Save your containers
Large plastic yogurt containers, baby food jars and clear plastic containers from the deli all come in handy when delivering food. Baby food jars are just the right size for delivering salad dressing. Larger containers can be used for fruit salad, gravy, salsa, etc. Transfer food to microwave-safe containers before reheating in the microwave.

Take it easy
You can do everything from scratch, even milk the cow, or you can take shortcuts like using frozen mashed potatoes, bread dough and pie crusts. After all, co-op cooking is supposed to make life easier.

Tip 7 - Don't prepare food that has to be eaten immediately, such as souffles

The best dishes to serve are those that improve with age. Italian food, soups, and stews are all good examples. One clue to look for: if the recipe says to "serve immediately," it may not be the best recipe to use.

Tip 8 - Take advantage of sales, buy in bulk, and invest in a freezer

Here is the real key to saving money with co-op cooking. Meat can be purchased in five to ten pound packages with a lower price per pound than with smaller packages. A freezer lets you take advantage of such sales. I buy meat when it's on sale, and then the next time we get together to fill out our six-week calendars, I look at what I have in the freezer and plan my menus accordingly.

Tip 9 - Have fun with your meals

Every now and then throw in the unexpected. Give Santa cookies at Christmas-time, or fortune cookies and disposable chopsticks with a Chinese stir-fry. You'll have fun thinking up ways to make your meals more enjoyable and your co-op families will have fun eating them.

At our house we have two choices for dinner — take it or leave it!

Chapter 5

Food Safety
(Or, how <u>not</u> to make your neighbors sick!)

The idea of cooking for several families each week can be intimidating. Even worse is the idea of giving your neighbors food poisoning. What a nightmare! More than 80 million Americans get sick from food poisoning every year, and there are more than two dozen organisms just waiting for a chance to add you to the list. That's the bad news. The good news is that you and your co-op friends won't have to give food-borne illness a second thought if you follow the simple rules in this chapter.

Rules for cooking safely

To prevent food poisoning it is important to know and follow the rules for proper food care and preparation.

The first rule is 1) keep everything in the kitchen **CLEAN** since most bacteria get into food through careless handling. Your goal is to keep "bugs" from getting into food and doing their dastardly deeds.

And, since most food poisoners can be controlled by cooking and refrigeration, the second and third rules are 2) keep food **HOT** or 3) **COLD**. Paying attention to the proper food temperature will deprive the ugly critters of the conditions they need to grow.

Keep your kitchen clean and safe

- **Everything that comes into contact with food should be clean**! Use dishwasher detergent and hot water to clean all surfaces and utensils. Don't forget to clean cabinet handles and can opener. Disinfect surfaces using a commercial product that contains bleach or prepare your own using one tablespoon chlorine bleach to one gallon of water.

- **Wash hands, counter tops, and utensils in hot, soapy water between each step in food preparation.** For example, if you take raw meat or poultry out to the barbecue, be sure to wash the plate well before putting the cooked food back on it. Bacteria present on raw meat and poultry can also get into other food if you're not careful to wash everything they've touched before exposing another food to the same surfaces and utensils. Raw food or items which need no further heating, such as fruits and vegetables, are particularly vulnerable.

- **Store foods in safe places.** Store frozen foods in the freezer, perishable food to be used within a few days in the refrigerator, and canned foods in a clean, dry place. Keep pets, household cleaners, and other chemicals away from food. Don't store food near leaky pipes or seeping moisture. Control household pests (flies, rats, mice, roaches).

- **Don't spread infection.** Always wash your hands well before beginning food preparation. If you take a bathroom break, change your baby's diaper, sneeze, blow your nose or scratch an itch, be sure to wash your hands again with soap and hot water. Use gloves to handle food if you have any kind of skin cut or infection on your hands. Don't sneeze or cough into food. If your hair is long, keep it tied back and don't comb or brush your hair in the kitchen. Don't use the same spoon more than once to taste food while preparing, cooking or serving food.

How to avoid food poisoning "bugs"...

- Get perishable foods into the refrigerator as quickly as possible after buying them.

- Wash raw fruits and vegetables thoroughly.

- Keep your kitchen clean.

- Wash your hands before preparing food.

- Keep hot foods hot and cold foods cold after they are prepared.

- NEVER LEAVE COOKED FOOD SITTING OUT UNLESS YOU PLAN TO EAT IT RIGHT AWAY — REFRIGERATE AS SOON AS POSSIBLE.

- **Keep washing and drying cloths clean.** Bacteria are present in towels and cloths you use over and over, so wash kitchen linens often. Throw out dirty or mildewed dish sponges. To sterilize a sponge, wash it in hot soapy water, and then, while it's wet, put it in a plastic bag and microwave on high for one minute.

- **Use plastic cutting boards for meat and poultry.** Plastic and other non-porous cutting boards are better for meat and poultry because you can wash them in the dishwasher. The hot soapy water will kill disease causing microbes. If you must use a wooden cutting board for meat, use it only for meat and sanitize it frequently with a solution of one tablespoon bleach in a gallon of hot water. Any cutting boards that have deep cuts or grooves should be replaced.

- **Wash the lids of canned foods before opening to keep dirt and bacteria from getting into the food.**

Keep hot food hot

- **Never leave cooked food sitting out unless you plan to eat it right away — refrigerate as soon as possible.** When cooked food is left out unheated, the possibility of bacterial growth is greater because the food quickly drops to room temperature where food poisoners thrive.

- **Cook thoroughly.** Use a meat thermometer to make sure that meat and poultry are cooked all the way through. Poultry juices should run clear. Insert the tip of the thermometer into the thickest part of the meat avoiding bone and fat. With whole poultry, insert the thermometer tip into the thickest part of the thigh next to the body. Cook meat and poultry to the temperatures shown in the chart at right.

- **Don't interrupt cooking.** Meat and poultry should be cooked completely at one time. Don't partially cook — bacterial growth could be encouraged.

- **Allow extra time for frozen food to cook.** It generally takes 1½ times the time required for thawed food to cook.

- **Thoroughly reheat leftovers.** Heat leftovers on the stove-top or in the microwave **rapidly** until hot (165° F internal temperature). Cover leftovers to retain moisture and ensure that food is heated throughout.

- **Reheat food only once.** Reheat only the amount of food that you and your family can eat at one sitting. Repeated heating and cooling of food can promote bacterial growth.

Cooking meat and poultry

When cooking meat and poultry, use a meat thermometer to make sure they are heated to the following temperatures:

	°F
Fresh Beef	
Rare	140
Medium	160
Well Done	170
Ground Beef	170
Fresh Veal	170
Fresh Lamb	
Medium	170
Well Done	180
Poultry	
Chicken	185
Turkey	185
Boneless turkey roast	175
Fresh Pork	160
Cured Pork	
Ham, raw	160
Ham, (fully cooked)	140
Shoulder (Cook before serving)	170

30 - Homemade To Go

Keep cold food cold

- **At the grocery store** make sure frozen foods are solid and that refrigerated foods feel cold. Pick up perishables last and — especially in hot weather — get them home and into the refrigerator quickly. Run other errands before buying groceries. If you live more than 30 minutes from the store, use an ice chest for the trip home.

- **Check your refrigerator and freezer temperatures.** Use a thermometer to check that your refrigerator is 40° F or slightly lower and your freezer is 0° F or colder.

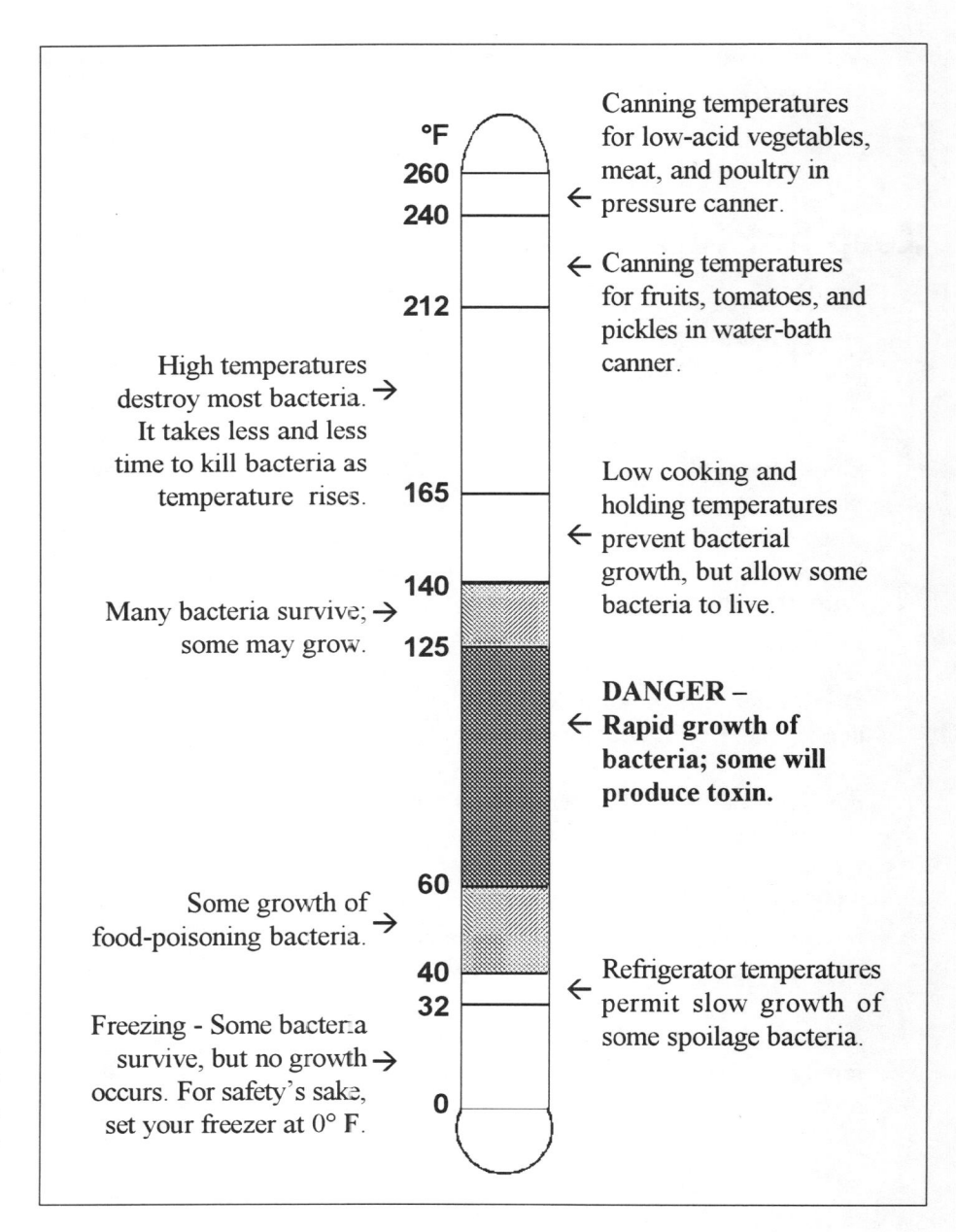

Bacteria:
How food temperature affects their growth

The figure at right shows the importance of keeping hot food hot — above 140° F, and cold food cold — below 40° F for refrigerated foods, and below 0° F for frozen items.

°F	
260	← Canning temperatures for low-acid vegetables, meat, and poultry in pressure canner.
240	
212	← Canning temperatures for fruits, tomatoes, and pickles in water-bath canner.
165	← Low cooking and holding temperatures prevent bacterial growth, but allow some bacteria to live.
140	
125	
	DANGER – ← **Rapid growth of bacteria; some will produce toxin.**
60	
40	← Refrigerator temperatures permit slow growth of some spoilage bacteria.
32	
0	

High temperatures destroy most bacteria. → It takes less and less time to kill bacteria as temperature rises.

Many bacteria survive; → some may grow.

Some growth of food-poisoning bacteria. →

Freezing - Some bacteria survive, but no growth → occurs. For safety's sake, set your freezer at 0° F.

- **Do not thaw frozen meat on the kitchen counter.** Instead, use one the following approved methods for thawing meat and poultry:

    Overnight in the refrigerator — Put frozen meat on a plate or larger container to catch drippings, and place on the bottom shelf in the refrigerator.

    In the microwave —
    1) Remove food from store wrap prior to microwave defrosting. (Foam and plastic wraps are not heat stable at high temperatures. Melting or warping from hot food may cause chemicals to migrate into food.)
    2) Cook meat and poultry immediately after micro-thawing.
    3) Remember to take food out of the microwave!

    In cold water — Put the frozen package in a watertight plastic bag under cold water. Change the water often. Cook or refrigerate as soon as it's thawed.

- **Cool cooked food quickly.** Don't let cooked food cool on the counter top. Divide large quantities, place in small shallow containers, cover loosely, and refrigerate immediately.

All these rules may seem a bit overwhelming at first, but will quickly become habit. Just remember — the old adage "rules are meant to be broken" does **not** apply when it comes to food safety!

Be an alert shopper

Carefully examine any canned food. Don't buy any dented or bulging cans. If the container has a safety seal, make sure it's intact. If the liquid in a jar is milky when it should be clear, don't buy it.

The "Sell by" and "Use by" dates printed on many products can be helpful in deciding whether food is still safe to buy. The "Sell by" date tells the grocer — and you, the consumer — how long the product should be kept for sale on the shelf. The "Use by" date is intended to tell you how long the product will retain top eating quality after you buy it.

Take allergies seriously!

Jane had been married just three weeks when she went to her in-laws for dinner. She told Margaret, her mother-in-law, that she was severely allergic to walnuts. Margaret believed that allergies were "all in people's heads" and that people use the allergy excuse to avoid eating foods they don't like.

For dessert Margaret made cookies. She told Jane she had used pecans when she had really used walnuts.

Not long after eating the cookies, Jane began to have trouble breathing. Her husband, Jim, immediately called an ambulance. After many harrowing hours in the hospital emergency room, she was stabilized and eventually allowed to go home.

Don't be like Margaret, please take allergies seriously.

For more information contact...

The Cooperative Extension Service — listed in local phone books under county government or State University. They answer food handling, nutrition and storage questions.

Food and Drug Administration — (800) 332-4010 *or* their web site at www.fda.gov. Contact them for up-to-date information on food safety and nutrition, and seafood storage and handling.

U.S. Department of Agriculture — call (800) 535-4555 to reach the USDA's Meat and Poultry Hotline. Call weekdays between 10 AM and 4 PM Eastern to speak to a specialist, or call anytime to hear recorded food safety messages. You can also write to "The Meat and Poultry Hotline," USDA-FSIS, Room 1180-S, Washington, D.C. 20250. They have many booklets available including the following:

- **Ground Meat and Ground Poultry**
- **Help, Power Outage!**
- **A Quick Consumer Guide to Safe Food Handling**
- **Safe Handling of Ready Prepared Holiday Turkey Dinners**
- **Take the Guesswork Out of Roasting a Turkey**
- **Take-Out Foods**
- **Use a Meat Thermometer—and Take the Guesswork Out of Cooking**

Nothing seems to make children more affectionate than sticky hands.

Chapter 6

Planning Your Meals

Some people seem to have a knack for menu planning and beautiful meal presentation. In our co-op Juanita has that extra special flair. Maybe it's because she's a florist or maybe she just has good taste, but when Juanita's meals arrive, we all agree they are as much fun to look at as to eat. We've learned a great deal from her about the art of meal planning. If you don't have the natural knack, then the next few pages will give you enough menu planning and presentation knowhow to create some "oohs" and "aahs" of your own.

Nutrition first

Sound nutrition is the foundation of every great meal. The U.S. Department of Agriculture's Food Guide Pyramid (below) can be a helpful tool in making nutritious choices for your menus. Our meal planning usually starts with a protein (meat, poultry, fish, and sometimes bean) main dish that often incorporates pasta or rice. Side dishes are chosen from the fruit or vegetable groups, and we frequently include some type of bread with the meal. Eating right means eating a wide variety of foods, and that's one of the benefits of co-op cooking. Families often have different food heritages. When you start sharing meals you'll be exposing each other to new foods. If everyone keeps an eye on the Food Guide Pyramid the variety in your meals will be both healthy and adventurous.

Make it appetizing!

Nutritious meals will have little benefit, however, if they aren't great tasting and great looking. That's where color, flavor, texture and temperature come into the meal planning equation.

- **Color:** Remember, your meal will be seen before it's eaten. Think of the dinner plate as a color palate. A colorful combination of foods is a feast for the eyes and sets the stage for a wonderful meal. Simple garnishes can add a lot. A sprig of parsley, lemon wedges, and radishes are classic and sometimes helpful, but browse through current food magazines for new

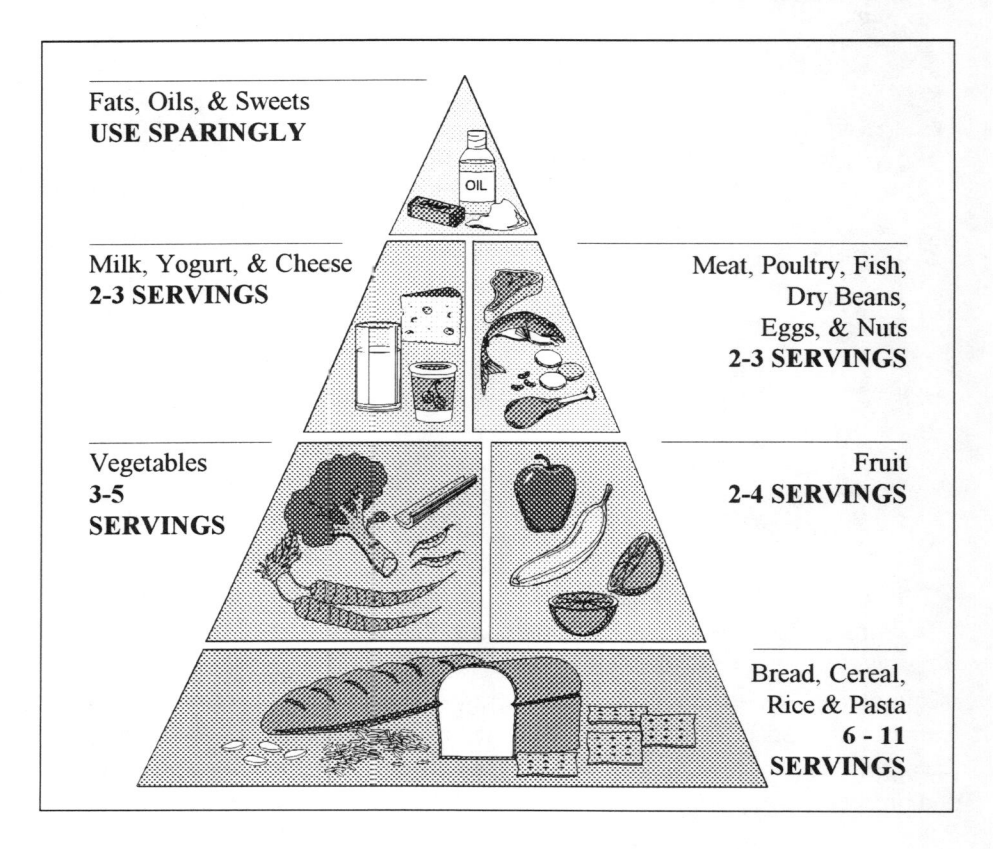

Food Guide Pyramid: *Use the Food Guide Pyramid when planning your meals. Eat a variety of foods each day, choosing from the foods in each group.*

Fats, Oils, & Sweets
USE SPARINGLY

Milk, Yogurt, & Cheese
2-3 SERVINGS

Meat, Poultry, Fish, Dry Beans, Eggs, & Nuts
2-3 SERVINGS

Vegetables
3-5 SERVINGS

Fruit
2-4 SERVINGS

Bread, Cereal, Rice & Pasta
6 - 11 SERVINGS

ideas. You'll often see dollops of bright and zippy salsas on broiled chicken breasts and fish, thin slices of red or yellow pepper making a colorful addition, or fresh herbs strategically sprinkled to add taste and eye appeal.

Most of the time you can give plenty of color appeal to your meals by simply selecting food combinations that complement each other and aren't monochromatic. For example, you wouldn't want to plan a meal of turkey breast, mashed potatoes and rolls. A green salad or steamed vegetables (as long as it isn't cauliflower) would make this meal more appetizing. Speaking of steamed vegetables, make sure they aren't overcooked or they will lose their color value. Properly cooked vegetables retain their bright color.

- **Flavor:** Another tip for great meal planning is to complement mild foods with spicier, more flavorful dishes. Give each menu some punch with an item that wakes up the taste buds, but don't overdo it. Most meals should consist of just one highly seasoned food. Balance is the key. Too many strong flavored foods can be just as unappetizing as too many bland dishes.

- **Texture:** Texture is another important factor to consider when choosing menu items. Meals are more interesting when they combine foods that are chewy, crunchy, and smooth. A meal of meat loaf, mashed potatoes and creamed corn would be greatly improved by substituting a crisp green salad for the creamed corn.

- **Food temperature and time of year:** The time of year will influence the temperature and types of foods you choose. On frigid winter evenings most of us enjoy a hearty stew with piping hot homemade bread and a small green salad, but the same meal falls flat in July. Summer meals are often lighter (salad might be the main dish) and cooler. Keep seasonal considerations in mind as you set out to create your co-op menus.

Use planning calendars

I highly recommend that your co-op put a menu planning calendar together. For your convenience blank planning calendars can be found in the appendix. Ask co-op members to bring a variety of menus to a brief meeting (we bring seven or eight menus each when we're putting together a six-week calendar). Plug in the menus on the appropriate days taking care to have a variety of foods each week. Finally, designate someone to make copies of the calendar for all the co-op members. This calendar will be so incredibly helpful you'll wonder how you ever got along without it.

Before co-op cooking, I was constantly vowing to get organized and plan menus weeks in advance. It never happened until our co-op got together and filled out a six-week menu calendar. What a great tool! I'm able to shop smarter (watch for specials on ingredients in upcoming dinners), avoid four chicken dinners in a row, and best of all, I always have an answer when the kids ask, "What's for dinner?"

The "kid factor"

Children and their special taste preferences may also play a role in your menu planning. If your co-op families include young children, there are some general do's and don'ts to consider. For example, most children under five like their food simple and straight forward. Grilled or broiled meat with vegetables on the side will usually be a bigger hit than a casserole. You might send vegetables uncooked so families can serve them raw or prepare them according to their youngsters' likes and dislikes. Go light on seasonings for the children's portions, and send toppings like sauces and gravies in separate containers. Of course, the foods children prefer change as they grow. That's why it's important to keep communication flowing between your co-op families.

With those thoughts in mind, I should mention that our co-op doesn't attempt to tailor every meal to our youngsters' tastes. We believe in expanding our children's food experiences, so we try to strike a balance between meals that are obvious kid pleasers and those that help them explore new tastes.

Menu ideas

On the following pages you will find 34 menus taken from our co-op calendars. We thought you might appreciate a few ideas just to get started. As you'll see, our co-op provides the main dish, a side dish, usually some kind of bread, and once in awhile (just for fun) dessert. That's how we organized the following menus, but of course, there are many other possibilities. Look in Chapter 7 for recipes marked with an asterisk (*).

Menu #1
Chicken Pie*
Green salad
Dinner rolls

Menu #2
Broiled Salmon Steaks*
Baked potatoes
Asparagus with Egg Sauce*

Menu #3
Beef Vegetable Stir-Fry*
White rice or Chinese noodles
Fresh Fruit Salad*

Menu #4
Chicken Enchiladas*
Shredded lettuce, salsa, sour cream
1 pint sorbet (per family)

Menu #5
Thick and Hearty Clam Chowder*
Bread bowls
Carrot sticks

Menu #6
Roast pork
Baked apples
Ore-Ida Cottage Fries

Menu #7
Moroccan Sandwiches*
Pita bread
Frozen Fruit Salad*

Menu #8
Meat loaf
Mashed Potatoes Florentine*
Dinner biscuits

Menu #9
Grilled chicken breasts
Louisiana Caviar* with tortilla chips
Melon balls

Menu #10
Italian Pasta Bake*
Caesar salad
French bread

Menu #11
Hawaiian Sausage Stir-Fry*
White rice
Chinese pea pods

Menu #12
Beef and Cabbage Braid (or variation)*
Waldorf Salad*
Homemade cookies or brownies

Menu #13
Asian Beef Kabobs*
White rice
Fresh Fruit*

Menu #14
Quiche
Spinach salad
Muffins

Menu #15
Ham slices
Creamy Au Gratin Potatoes*
Steamed broccoli

Menu #16
Chili
Johnny Cake*
Fresh Fruit Salad*

Menu #17
Roast turkey breast
Gourmet Mashed Potatoes*
Green Beans with Almonds*

Menu #18
Barbecue Beef Cups*
Tomato and Avocado Salad*
Company Fruit Salad*

Menu #19
South of the Border Pork Tenderloin*
Festive Rice*
Heavenly Grapes*

Menu #20
Chicken Parmigiana*
Green salad
Bread sticks

Menu #21
Cream of Tomato Soup*
Assorted raw vegetable sticks
Aunt Babe's Onion Bread*

Menu #22
Grilled hamburgers
Ore-Ida French Fries
Coleslaw*

Menu #23
Chicken Pasta Medley*
Sourdough rolls
Brownies

Menu #24
Spicy Skillet Pork*
White rice
Green salad

Menu #25
Crock-Pot Roast*
(with Vegetables)
Crescent rolls

Menu #26
Spaghetti Sauce with Meat*
Green salad
Cheesy French Bread*

Menu #27
Pork Chop and Potato Casserole*
Stewed Apples*
Green beans

Menu #28
Vegetarian Chimichangas*
Tortilla chips and salsa
Cantaloupe chunks

Menu #29
Barbecue Beef Tri-Tip*
Marinated Tomatoes*
Potato rolls

Menu #30
Shrimp-and-Pasta Salad*
Fresh Fruit Salad*
Muffins

Menu #31
Cheese Ravioli with Marinara*
Antipasto Salad*
Nutty Rum Ice Cream*

Menu #32
Fish Fillets on Rice*
Petit peas
Peach slices

Menu #33
Pork Loin Roll-Ups*
Cooked carrots
Rice Pilaf*

Menu #34
Grilled steak
Tangy Vegetable Potato Salad*
Hard rolls

"Give what you have to someone; it may be better than you dare to think."
—HENRY WADSWORTH LONGFELLOW

Chapter 7

Recipes

The real fun of co-op cooking is about to begin. We've already done the multiplying for you in the following recipes. Each dish is offered in its traditional 4 to 6 serving size and then we've bumped each recipe up to 24 or more servings.

On some recipes you will notice special last minute preparation instructions for co-op families. You will want to write these instructions on dinner tags found in the appendix and deliver them with your meals.

Spaghetti Sauce with Meat

Servings (1 cup per serving)	6	12	18	24	30	36
lean ground beef	¼ lb.	½ lb.	¾ lb.	1 lb.	1¼ lb.	1½ lb.
Italian sausage	¼ lb.	½ lb.	¾ lb.	1 lb.	1¼ lb.	1½ lb.
olive oil	½ Tbsp	1 Tbsp	1½ Tbsp	2 Tbsp	2½ Tbsp	3 Tbsp
green bell peppers, diced	½ cup	1 cup	1½ cups	2 cups	2½ cups	3 cups
onions, chopped	½ cup	1 cup	1½ cups	2 cups	2½ cups	3 cups
tomato sauce, 28-oz. cans	1 can	2 cans	3 cans	4 cans	5 cans	6 cans
tomato paste	3 oz.	6 oz.	9 oz.	12 oz.	15 oz.	18 oz.
sliced mushrooms	½ cup	1 cup	1½ cups	2 cups	2½ cups	3 cups
dried parsley flakes	1 Tbsp	1½ Tbsp	2 Tbsp + a scant tsp	3 Tbsp	¼ cup	¼ cup + ½ Tbsp
dried oregano	1 tsp	½ Tbsp	2¼ tsp	1 Tbsp	1 Tbsp + a scant tsp	1½ Tbsp
cloves garlic, crushed	1	2	3	4	5	6
black pepper	⅛ tsp	¼ tsp	¼ tsp	¼ + ⅛ tsp	½ tsp	½ tsp
spaghetti, 12-oz. packages (deliver uncooked)	1 pkg.	2 pkg.	3 pkg.	4 pkg.	5 pkg.	6 pkg.

In a large pot cook meat; drain fat. Return to heat and add remaining ingredients except for spaghetti. Bring to a boil, reduce heat and simmer for 2 hours stirring occasionally.

Instructions for co-op families: Cook spaghetti according to package directions. Heat sauce and serve on spaghetti.

Cheesy French Bread

Loaves	1	2	3	4	5	6
loaf French or Italian bread	1	2	3	4	5	6
butter or margarine	¼ cup	½ cup	¾ cup	1 cup	1¼ cups	1½ cups
freshly grated Parmesan cheese	⅓ cup	⅔ cup	1 cup	1⅓ cups	1⅔ cups	2 cups

Cut loaves in half lengthwise. Melt butter or margarine; brush on bread halves. Reshape loaves and wrap in aluminum foil. Put Parmesan cheese in plastic bags.

Instructions for co-op families: Preheat oven to 450° F. Unwrap bread and place butter side up on cookie sheet. Sprinkle with Parmesan cheese; bake for 8 minutes or until golden brown.

Beef Vegetable Stir-Fry

Servings	6	12	18	24	30	36
Partially frozen sirloin steak (thinly sliced)	1 pound	2 pounds	3 pounds	4 pounds	5 pounds	6 pounds
cornstarch	1 Tbsp	2 Tbsp	3 Tbsp	¼ cup	¼ cup + 1 Tbsp	¼ cup + 2 Tbsp
vegetable oil	2 Tbsp	¼ cup	¼ cup + 2 Tbsp	½ cup	½ cup + 2 Tbsp	¾ cup
frozen stir-fry vegetables (broccoli, carrots, water chestnuts)	1 1-lb bag	2 1-lb bags	3 1-lb bags	4 1-lb bags	5 1-lb bags	6 1-lb bags

Marinade:

water	¼ cup	½ cup	¾ cup	1 cup	1¼ cups	1½ cups
soy sauce	⅓ cup	⅔ cup	1 cup	1⅓ cups	1⅔ cups	2 cups
brown sugar	2 Tbsp	¼ cup	¼ cup + 2 Tbsp	½ cup	½ cup + 2 Tbsp	¾ cup
sherry	3 Tbsp	¼ cup + 2 Tbsp	½ cup + 1 Tbsp	¾ cup	¾ cup + 3 Tbsp	1 cup + 2 Tbsp
garlic, minced	1 clove	2 cloves	3 cloves	4 cloves	5 cloves	6 cloves
ground ginger	1 tsp	2 tsp	1 Tbsp	1 Tbsp + 1 tsp	1 Tbsp + 2 tsp	2 Tbsp

Mix marinade ingredients together. Place half of the marinade and the steak in a glass container. Cover and refrigerate for one to eight hours. Mix cornstarch with remaining marinade; refrigerate.

Micro-cook frozen stir-fry vegetables, one package at a time, until tender-crisp. Put into co-op dishes.

Remove steak from the marinade; discard marinade. Cook meat in hot oil, a few pieces at a time, just until done. Drain fat. Add reserved marinade to pan; cook and stir until thickened and bubbly. Spoon meat and marinade over vegetables.

Barbecue Beef Tri-Tip

You can also use your favorite homemade marinade.

Servings	6	12	18	24	30	36
beef tri-tip roast	2 pounds	4 pounds	6 pounds	8 pounds	10 pounds	12 pounds
meat marinade mix, 1½-oz pkg	1 pkg	2 pkgs	2 pkgs	3 pkgs	4 pkgs	4 pkgs

Prepare meat marinade according to package instructions and place in a shallow glass pan. Pierce meat surfaces with a fork; add to marinade. Allow to stand for 15 minutes, or according to package instructions, turning frequently.

Remove meat from marinade and cook to desired doneness on a gas or charcoal grill following the instructions that came with your grill. Brush with marinade while cooking.

Beef and Cabbage Braid

Loaves (4 to 6 servings each)	1 loaf	2 loaves	3 loaves	4 loaves	5 loaves	6 loaves
frozen bread dough	1 loaf	2 loaves	3 loaves	4 loaves	5 loaves	6 loaves
onion, diced	1 cup	2 cups	3 cups	4 cups	5 cups	6 cups
lean ground beef	½ pound	1 pound	1½ pounds	2 pounds	2½ pounds	3 pounds
green cabbage, thinly sliced	2 cups	4 cups	6 cups	8 cups	10 cups	12 cups
salt	½ tsp	1 tsp	½ Tbsp	2 tsp	2½ tsp	1 Tbsp
black pepper	⅛ tsp	¼ tsp	¼ + ⅛ tsp	½ tsp	½ + ⅛ tsp	½ + ¼ tsp
flour	1 Tbsp	2 Tbsp	3 Tbsp	4 Tbsp	5 Tbsp	6 Tbsp
Swiss cheese, sliced	¼ pound	½ pound	¾ pound	1 pound	1¼ pounds	1½ pounds
egg	1	1	1	1	1	1
caraway seeds (optional)	1 tsp	2 tsp	1 Tbsp	1 Tbsp + 1 tsp	1 Tbsp + 2 tsp	2 Tbsp

Thaw bread dough following package instructions. Let rise until double in bulk and punch down. Lightly grease a jelly roll pan or cookie sheet. Prepare filling.

Filling: Cook ground beef and onions on high heat until the meat loses it pink color. Drain excess fat. Stir in cabbage; reduce heat, cover and cook until cabbage is limp, about 10 to 15 minutes. Stir in salt, pepper and flour. Cook and stir one minute more. Remove from heat.

Shape braids following directions below using about 2¼ cups of filling and ¼ pound cheese for each braid. Place braids on cookie sheet. Beat egg with 1 Tbsp water and brush on loaves; sprinkle with caraway seeds. Bake at 350° F for 25 minutes or until golden brown. *Note: Two braids fit on a standard-sized cookie sheet. While you are baking the first batch, prepare the next braids for baking.*

Reuben Braid: Prepare as above except for filling use ½ pound pastrami, ¼ pound Swiss cheese, and 1½ cups well-drained sauerkraut.

Steak and Cheese Braid: Prepare as above except for filling use ½ pound thinly sliced cooked roast beef, ¼ pound Swiss cheese, and 1 cup sautéed onions (optional). Omit caraway seeds.

Ham and Cheese Braid: Prepare as above except for filling use ½ pound thinly sliced or cubed ham and ¼ pound Swiss cheese. Substitute sesame seeds for the caraway seeds.

Directions for shaping braids:

1.) Roll bread dough into a rectangle about 14" x 10". Arrange filling down the center third.

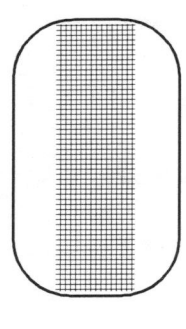

2.) Using clean kitchen scissors, cut 1" to 1½" wide slits along each long side.

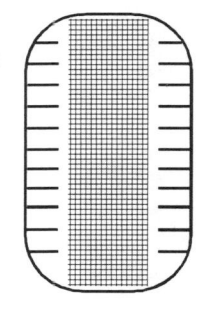

3.) Starting at one end, fold strips at an angle across the filling, alternating from side to side.

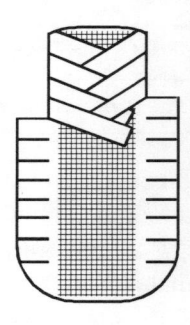

Barbecue Beef Cups

Servings (2 per serving)	4	8	12	16	20	24
frozen roll dough	8	16	24	32	40	48
lean ground beef	¾ pound	1½ pounds	2¼ pounds	3 pounds	3¾ pounds	4½ pounds
chopped onions	¼ cup	½ cup	¾ cup	1 cup	1¼ cups	1½ cups
barbecue sauce	⅓ cup	⅔ cup	1 cup	1⅓ cups	1⅔ cups	2 cups
shredded cheddar cheese	½ cup	1 cup	1½ cups	2 cups	2½ cups	3 cups

Thaw roll dough following package instructions. Cook ground meat and onion until the meat is no longer pink. Drain fat. Add barbecue sauce, stir and cook for one minute more. Remove from heat and set aside.

Lightly grease muffin cups (you'll want to borrow muffin tins from your co-op families). Flatten thawed roll dough into 5" rounds; press into the bottom and sides of muffin cups. Put about ¼ cup of the meat mixture into each of the dough-lined cups. Top with shredded cheddar cheese. Bake 15 to 20 minutes at 350° F or until rolls are brown.

Crock-Pot Roast

Have your co-op members drop off their crock-pots on your cooking day for this easy and delicious meal.

Servings	6	12	18	24	30	36
beef pot roast, about 2 lb. each	1	2	3	4	5	6
Idaho potatoes	4	8	12	16	20	24
carrots	3	6	9	12	15	18
onion soup mix	1 pkg	2 pkg	3 pkg	4 pkg	5 pkg	6 pkg
tomato sauce, 8-oz. cans	1	2	3	4	5	6
dry red wine (or red wine vinegar)	¼ cup	½ cup	¾ cup	1 cup	1¼ cups	1½ cups
Worcestershire sauce	2 tsp	1 Tbsp + 1 tsp	2 Tbsp	2 Tbsp + 2 tsp	3 Tbsp + 1 tsp	¼ cup
garlic powder	⅛ tsp	¼ tsp	¼ + ⅛ tsp	½ tsp	½ + ⅛ tsp	½ + ¼ tsp

Place one beef pot roast into each crock-pot. Cut up carrots and potatoes and divide into crock-pots. Sprinkle one package of onion soup mix, one can tomato sauce, ¼ cup dry red wine (or red wine vinegar), 2 tsp Worcestershire sauce, and ⅛ tsp garlic powder over each roast.

Cover and cook on low 8 to 10 hours. Deliver meals in crock-pots.

Asian Beef Kabobs

Servings	4	8	12	16	20	24
well-trimmed boneless beef top sirloin steak, 1" thick	1 pound	2 pounds	3 pounds	4 pounds	5 pounds	6 pounds
green onions cut into 1½" pieces	6	12	18	24	30	36

Marinade:

packed brown sugar	¼ cup	½ cup	¾ cup	1 cup	1¼ cups	1½ cups
dry sherry	3 Tbsp	¼ cup + 2 Tbsp	½ cup + 1 Tbsp	¾ cup	¾ cup + 3 Tbsp	1 cup + 2 Tbsp
soy sauce	3 Tbsp	¼ cup + 2 Tbsp	½ cup + 1 Tbsp	¾ cup	¾ cup + 3 Tbsp	1 cup + 2 Tbsp
dark sesame oil	2 tsp	1 Tbsp + 1 tsp	2 Tbsp	2 Tbsp + 2 tsp	3 Tbsp + 1 tsp	¼ cup
cloves garlic, crushed	2	4	6	8	10	12
ground ginger	½ tsp	1 tsp	½ Tbsp	2 tsp	2½ tsp	1 Tbsp

Cut steak crosswise into ¼" thick strips. Combine marinade ingredients. Place beef and half of the marinade in plastic bag, turning to coat; close securely. Marinate in refrigerator 20 minutes; reserve remaining marinade.

Meanwhile soak 6" bamboo skewers (4 per serving) in water 10 minutes; drain. Remove beef from marinade; discard marinade. Alternately thread beef (weaving back and forth) and green onion onto skewers.

Place kabobs on rack in broiler pan so surface of kabobs is 3 to 4" from heat. Broil 5 to 6 minutes, turning once. Brush kabobs with reserved marinade during last 2 minutes.

Source of original recipe: The Idaho Beef Council

Italian Pasta Bake

Servings	4	8	12	16	20	24
pasta (rotini, ziti or mostaccioli)	½ pound	1 pound	1½ pounds	2 pounds	2½ pounds	3 pounds
Italian sausage	½ pound	1 pound	1½ pounds	2 pounds	2½ pounds	3 pounds
pasta sauce, 26-ounce jars	1	2	3	4	5	6
shredded mozzarella cheese (divided)	2 cups	4 cups (1 lb)	6 cups	8 cups (2 lb)	10 cups	12 cups (3 lb)
chopped parsley	1 Tbsp	2 Tbsp	3 Tbsp	¼ cup	¼ cup + 1 Tbsp	¼ cup + 2 Tbsp

Brown sausage and drain fat. Prepare pasta according to directions on package and drain. In large bowl combine pasta, sausage, and pasta sauce with half of the cheese. Pour mixture into lightly greased co-op dishes. Cover and bake 30 minutes at 350° F. Uncover; top with remaining cheese and sprinkle with parsley. Bake 10-15 minutes longer.

Spicy Skillet Pork
Serve over hot cooked rice.

Servings	4	8	12	16	20	24
vegetable oil	2 Tbsp	¼ cup	¼ cup + 2 Tbsp	½ cup	½ cup + 2 Tbsp	¾ cup
boneless pork sirloin, cubed	1 pound	2 pounds	3 pounds	4 pounds	5 pounds	6 pounds
taco seasoning mix (there are about 4 Tbsp per 1.25 oz. pkg)	2 Tbsp	3 tbsp	¼ cup	¼ cup + 2 Tbsp	½ cup	½ cup + 1 Tbsp
mild chunky style salsa	1 cup	2 cups	3 cups	4 cups	5 cups	6 cups
peach preserves	½ cup	1 cup	1½ cups	2 cups	2½ cups	3 cups

Brown pork cubes in hot oil a few at a time. Drain excess fat. Return meat to pan and add taco seasoning mix, salsa and peach preserves; stir well. Lower heat and simmer, covered, for about 20 minutes.

Hawaiian Sausage Stir-Fry
Serve over hot cooked rice.

Servings	4	8	12	16	20	24
cornstarch	1 Tbsp	2 Tbsp	3 Tbsp	¼ cup	¼ cup + 1 Tbsp	¼ cup + 2 Tbsp
ground ginger	¼ tsp	½ tsp	½ + ¼ tsp	1 tsp	1¼ tsp	½ Tbsp
cider vinegar	1 Tbsp	2 Tbsp	3 Tbsp	¼ cup	¼ cup + 1 Tbsp	¼ cup + 2 Tbsp
soy sauce	1 Tbsp	2 Tbsp	3 Tbsp	¼ cup	¼ cup + 1 Tbsp	¼ cup + 2 Tbsp
apricot preserves	½ cup	1 cup	1½ cups	2 cups	2½ cups	3 cups
green pepper, sliced	1	2	3	4	5	6
onion, sliced	1 cup	2 cups	3 cups	4 cups	5 cups	6 cups
kielbasa or smoked sausage, sliced ¾" thick	1 pound	2 pounds	3 pounds	4 pounds	5 pounds	6 pounds
vegetable oil	1 Tbsp	2 Tbsp	3 Tbsp	¼ cup	¼ cup + 1 Tbsp	¼ cup + 2 Tbsp
pineapple chunks, drained	1 cup	2 cups	3 cups	4 cups	5 cups	6 cups

Combine cornstarch and ground ginger in a bowl. Add vinegar, soy sauce, and preserves. Set this sauce aside.
    Sauté green pepper, onion and sausage in hot oil until the vegetables are barely tender. Add the sauce and cook until thickened. Stir in pineapple chunks and heat.

Pork Loin Roll-Ups

Servings	4	8	12	16	20	24
boneless center pork loin slices (4 per pound)	1 pound	2 pounds	3 pounds	4 pounds	5 pounds	6 pounds
red bell pepper, cut into strips	½	1	1½	2	2½	3
green bell pepper, cut into strips	½	1	1½	2	2½	3
vegetable oil	1 Tbsp	2 Tbsp	3 Tbsp	¼ cup	¼ cup + 1 Tbsp	¼ cup + 2 Tbsp
orange juice	⅔ cup	1⅓ cups	2 cups	2⅔ cups	3⅓ cups	4 cups
barbecue sauce	⅔ cup	1⅓ cups	2 cups	2⅔ cups	3⅓ cups	4 cups
Deli-style mustard	1 Tbsp	2 Tbsp	3 Tbsp	¼ cup	¼ cup + 1 Tbsp	¼ cup + 2 Tbsp

Pound pork slices to about ¼ inch thick. Place a few red and green pepper strips on each pork slice. Roll up and use toothpicks to secure.

Brown pork rolls in hot oil. Drain fat. Combine orange juice, barbecue sauce, and mustard; add to pork rolls in pan. Bring to a boil. Reduce heat, cover and simmer 10 to 12 minutes. Remove toothpicks before serving.

South of the Border Pork Tenderloin

Servings	6	12	18	24	30	36
pork tenderloin	1½ pounds	3 pounds	4½ pounds	6 pounds	7½ pounds	9 pounds
ground cumin	1 tsp	2 tsp	1 Tbsp	1 Tbsp + 1 tsp	1 Tbsp + 2 tsp	2 Tbsp
chili powder	1 tsp	2 tsp	1 Tbsp	1 Tbsp + 1 tsp	1 Tbsp + 2 tsp	2 Tbsp
oregano	½ tsp	1 tsp	½ Tbsp	2 tsp	2½ tsp	1 Tbsp
garlic powder	¼ tsp	½ tsp	½ + ¼ tsp	1 tsp	1¼ tsp	½ Tbsp
salt	¼ tsp	½ tsp	½ + ¼ tsp	1 tsp	1¼ tsp	½ Tbsp
black pepper	¼ tsp	½ tsp	½ + ¼ tsp	1 tsp	1¼ tsp	½ Tbsp
ground red pepper	⅛ tsp	¼ tsp	¼ + ⅛ tsp	½ tsp	½ + ⅛ tsp	½ + ¼ tsp

Preheat oven to 375° F. Combine all ingredients except for the pork tenderloin. Rub the spices into the tenderloin until evenly coated. Place on a rack in a shallow, lightly greased baking pan. Insert a meat thermometer into the thickest part of the largest piece of meat. Bake until the thermometer reads 160° F, about 45 minutes. Slice thinly across the grain before serving.

Pork Chop and Potato Casserole

Servings	6	12	18	24	30	36
pork chops	6	12	18	24	30	36
green onions, chopped	4	8	12	16	20	24
10¾-ounce can condensed cream of mushroom soup	1 can	2 cans	3 cans	4 cans	5 cans	6 cans
milk	⅔ cup	1⅓ cups	2 cups	2⅔ cups	3⅓ cups	4 cups
potatoes, peeled and sliced	3	6	9	12	15	18
American cheese slices	6	12	18	24	30	36

Brown pork chops and set aside. Sauté green onions in the drippings. Add soup and milk and mix well. Layer potato slices in lightly greased casseroles. Cover potatoes with cheese slices. Place pork chops on top of cheese and potatoes. Pour the soup and onion mixture over the pork chops. Bake, covered, for 50 minutes at 350° F. Uncover and bake 15 minutes more. *Note: Six servings fit into a 9" x 13" inch casserole dish.*

Chicken Enchiladas

Servings	6	12	18	24	30	36
boneless chicken breast, cooked and shredded	1 pound	2 pounds	3 pounds	4 pounds	5 pounds	6 pounds
monterey jack cheese, shredded	1 cup	2 cups	3 cups	4 cups	5 cups	6 cups
cheddar cheese, shredded	1 cup	2 cups	3 cups	4 cups	5 cups	6 cups
fresh chives, snipped	½ cup	1 cup	1½ cups	2 cups	2½ cups	3 cups
garlic, minced	½ tsp	1 tsp	½ Tbsp	2 tsp	2½ tsp	1 Tbsp
ground cumin	½ tsp	1 tsp	½ Tbsp	2 tsp	2½ tsp	1 Tbsp
ground black pepper	¼ tsp	½ tsp	½ + ¼ tsp	1 tsp	1¼ tsp	½ Tbsp
enchilada sauce, 29-ounce can	1 can	2 cans	3 cans	4 cans	5 cans	6 cans
6" corn tortillas	12	24	36	48	60	72
sliced black olives, 2-oz. can	1 can	2 cans	3 cans	4 cans	5 cans	6 cans

Mix together the chicken, half of the monterey jack cheese, half of the cheddar cheese, half of the chives, the garlic, cumin and black pepper; set aside.

Spread ½ cup of the enchilada sauce in the bottom of each rectangular co-op casserole or 13 x 9 inch pan. Transfer some of the remaining sauce to a large skillet and heat. To soften the tortillas, submerge them one at a time in the sauce. Shake off the excess sauce and transfer to a plate. Put about ¼ cup of the chicken filling down the middle of each tortilla and roll up. Place seam side down in the pan. Pour remaining sauce over the filled tortillas; top with remaining cheeses, chives, and olives. Cover with foil and bake for 30 minutes at 350° F.

Chicken Pie

Pies (each serves 6)	1	2	3	4	5	6
homemade or frozen pie crust	1	2	3	4	5	6
vegetable oil	2 Tbsp	¼ cup	6 Tbsp	½ cup	⅔ cup	¾ cup
onion, chopped	½ cup	1 cup	1½ cups	2 cups	2½ cups	3 cups
green pepper, chopped	2 Tbsp	¼ cup	6 Tbsp	½ cup	⅔ cup	¾ cup
flour	2 Tbsp	¼ cup	6 Tbsp	½ cup	⅔ cup	¾ cup
chicken broth	½ cup	1 cup	1½ cup	2 cups	2½ cups	3 cups
boneless chicken breast, cooked and cubed	1 pound	2 pounds	3 pounds	4 pounds	5 pounds	6 pounds
diced canned carrots, drained	¾ cup	1½ cups	2¼ cups	3 cups	3¾ cups	4½ cups
salt	¼ tsp	½ tsp	½ + ¼ tsp	1 tsp	1¼ tsp	½ Tbsp
egg, beaten slightly	1	2	3	4	5	6
American cheese slices	6	12	13	24	30	36

Preheat oven to 425° F. Thaw pie crust if frozen. Prick the pie crust all over with a fork and bake for 8 minutes. Remove from oven; lower oven temperature to 400° F.

Sauté onions and green pepper in oil until limp but not brown. Sprinkle with flour; stir until well blended. Add chicken broth; stir and cook until thickened. Remove from heat. Add chicken, carrots, salt and egg. Mix well. Turn into cooked pie crust; top with cheese. Bake 20 to 25 minutes or until cheese is melted and the pie is heated through.

Chicken Pasta Medley

Servings	6	12	18	24	30	36
alfredo sauce mix	2 pkgs	4 pkgs	6 pkgs	8 pkgs	10 pkgs	12 pkgs
fresh linguini	1 pound	2 pounds	3 pounds	4 pounds	5 pounds	6 pounds
frozen vegetable mix (broccoli, cauliflower, carrots)	1 1-lb bag	2 1-lb bags	3 1-lb bags	4 1-lb bags	5 1-lb bags	6 1-lb bags
chicken breasts, skinned, boned, cut in small pieces	1½ pounds	3 pounds	4½ pounds	6 pounds	7½ pounds	9 pounds
olive oil or butter	¼ cup	½ cup	¾ cup	1 cup	1¼ cups	1½ cups
fresh basil, snipped	1 Tbsp	2 Tbsp	3 Tbsp	¼ cup	¼ cup + 1 Tbsp	¼ cup + 2 Tbsp
garlic cloves, minced	2	4	6	8	10	12

Make alfredo sauce according to package directions. Cook linguini as directed on package. Toss linguini with alfredo sauce and divide among co-op dishes; set aside.

Micro-cook frozen vegetables, one bag at a time, until tender-crisp. Meanwhile, in large skillet or wok, stir-fry chicken in olive oil or butter with basil and garlic until done. Place vegetables and chicken over noodles.

Moroccan Sandwiches

Servings	4	8	12	16	20	24
olive oil	2 tsp	1 Tbsp + 1 tsp	2 Tbsp	2 Tbsp + 2 tsp	3 Tbsp + 1 tsp	¼ cup
cider vinegar	1½ Tbsp	3 Tbsp	¼ cup + ½ Tbsp	¼ cup + 2 Tbsp	¼ cup + 3½ Tbsp	½ cup + 1 Tbsp
oregano leaves	¼ tsp	½ tsp	½ + ¼ tsp	1 tsp	1¼ tsp	½ Tbsp
dried mint leaves	¼ tsp	½ tsp	½ + ¼ tsp	1 tsp	1¼ tsp	½ Tbsp
salt	⅛ tsp	¼ tsp	¼ + ⅛ tsp	½ tsp	½ + ⅛ tsp	½ + ¼ tsp
boneless chicken, cooked & cubed	1 pound	2 pounds	3 pounds	4 pounds	5 pounds	6 pounds
sweet onions, sliced	⅓ cup	⅔ cup	1 cup	1⅓ cups	1⅔ cups	2 cups
cucumber, diced	⅔ cup	1⅓ cups	2 cups	2⅔ cups	3⅓ cups	4 cups
chopped tomatoes	1 cup	2 cups	3 cups	4 cups	5 cups	6 cups
whole lettuce leaves	8	16	24	32	40	48
whole pita breads, halved	4	8	12	16	20	24

In a large bowl combine olive oil, vinegar, oregano, mint leaves and salt. Add chicken, onions, cucumber, and tomatoes. Toss gently. Divide among co-op dishes. Wash lettuce leaves and put into plastic bags for each family.
Instructions for co-op families: Place a lettuce leaf into a pita bread half. Top with chicken and vegetable mixture.

Chicken Parmigiana

Servings	4	8	12	16	20	24
boneless chicken breast halves	4	8	12	16	20	24
eggs	1	2	3	4	5	6
milk	2 Tbsp	¼ cup	¼ cup + 2 Tbsp	¾ cup	½ cup + 2 Tbsp	¾ cup
seasoned bread crumbs	1 cup	2 cups	3 cups	4 cups	5 cups	6 cups
margarine	2 Tbsp	¼ cup	¼ cup + 2 Tbsp	¾ cup	½ cup + 2 Tbsp	¾ cup
spaghetti sauce, 16-oz. jar	1 jar	2 jars	3 jars	4 jars	5 jars	6 jars
Swiss cheese slices	4	8	12	16	20	24
slices mozzarella cheese	4	8	12	16	20	24
Parmesan cheese	1 Tbsp	2 Tbsp	3 Tbsp	¼ cup	¼ cup + 1 Tbsp	¼ cup + 2 Tbsp

Pound chicken breast halves until thin. Dip in beaten egg and milk. Roll in bread crumbs; sauté in margarine. Layer bottom of co-op casseroles with half of the spaghetti sauce, chicken breasts, Swiss cheese and mozzarella cheese. Top with remaining sauce; sprinkle with Parmesan cheese. Bake for 30 minutes at 350° F.

Cheese Ravioli with Marinara

Servings	5	10	15	20	25	30
frozen Rosetto Cheese Ravioli, 24-25-oz. package	1 pkg.	2 pkg.	3 pkg.	4 pkg.	5 pkg.	6 pkg.
small onion, chopped	1	2	3	4	5	6
olive oil	1 Tbsp	2 Tbsp	3 Tbsp	¼ cup	¼ cup + 1 Tbsp	¼ cup + 2 Tbsp
canned diced tomatoes with Italian seasoning, undrained	1 14½-oz. can	2 14½-oz. cans	3 14½-oz. cans	4 14½-oz. cans	5 14½-oz. cans	6 14½-oz. cans
Italian style tomato paste	6 oz.	12 oz.	18 oz.	24 oz.	30 oz.	36 oz.
water	½ cup	1 cup	1½ cups	2 cups	2½ cups	3 cups
sugar (optional)	½ tsp	1 tsp	½ Tbsp	2 tsp	2½ tsp	1 Tbsp

Sauce: Cook onion in hot olive oil until tender. Add tomatoes and tomato paste. Stir in water; blend well. Stir in sugar (if desired); salt and pepper to taste; heat through.

Cook frozen Rosetto Cheese Ravioli according to package directions. Divide among co-op dishes; top with sauce.

Vegetarian Chimichangas

Servings	6	12	18	24	30	36
pinto beans, 29-oz. can	1 can	2 cans	3 cans	4 cans	5 cans	6 cans
diced green chiles, 7-oz. can	1 can	2 cans	3 cans	4 cans	5 cans	6 cans
sliced black olives, 4-oz. can	1 can	2 cans	3 cans	4 cans	5 cans	6 cans
shredded cabbage	1½ cups	3 cups	4½ cups	6 cups	7½ cups	9 cups
shredded carrot	¼ cup	½ cup	¾ cup	1 cup	1¼ cups	1½ cups
shredded sharp cheddar cheese	1 cup	2 cups	3 cups	4 cups	5 cups	6 cups
salsa (divided)	2 cups	4 cups	6 cups	8 cups	10 cups	12 cups
10" flour tortillas	12	24	32	48	60	72
sour cream	1 cup	2 cups	3 cups	4 cups	5 cups	6 cups
sliced green onions	¼ cup	½ cup	¾ cup	1 cup	1¼ cups	1½ cups

Rinse and drain beans. Combine beans, chiles, olives, cabbage, carrots, cheese, and half of the salsa in a bowl. (Put remaining salsa in containers for delivery). Wrap tortillas in a clean cloth towel and microwave for 1-2 minutes. Lay tortillas flat and place about ½ cup of the bean mixture in a strip near the edge. Fold ends in and roll up tightly. Place filled tortillas seam side down in lightly greased co-op dishes. Put sour cream and onions in containers for delivery.

Instructions for co-op families: Just before serving bake at 425° F. for about 15 minutes until lightly browned. Serve with sour cream, salsa, and green onions.

Broiled Salmon Steaks (with Lemon Dill Sauce)

Servings	4	8	12	16	20	24
salmon steaks, 1" thick	1½ pounds	3 pounds	4½ pounds	6 pounds	7½ pounds	9 pounds
butter or margarine, melted	2 Tbsp	¼ cup	¼ cup + 2 Tbsp	½ cup	½ cup + 2 Tbsp	¾ cup
lemon juice	1 Tbsp	2 Tbsp	3 Tbsp	¼ cup	¼ cup + 1 Tbsp	¼ cup + 2 Tbsp
dried dillweed, crushed	½ tsp	1 tsp	½ Tbsp	2 tsp	2½ tsp	1 Tbsp
pepper	dash	⅛ tsp	⅛ tsp	¼ tsp	¼ tsp	¼ + ⅛ tsp

Lemon Dill Sauce: Melt butter or margarine; stir in lemon juice, dillweed and pepper.

Place steaks on greased rack of broiler pan. Brush with Lemon Dill Sauce. Broil 4 inches from heat for 5 minutes. Turn steaks, brush with sauce, and broil 3 to 7 minutes more or until fish flakes easily with a fork.

Fish Fillets on Rice

Servings	4	8	12	16	20	24
fish fillets, fresh or frozen	1 pound	2 pounds	3 pounds	4 pounds	5 pounds	6 pounds
long grain rice, uncooked	½ cup	1 cup	1½ cups	2 cups	2½ cups	3 cups
onions, chopped	¼ cup	½ cup	¾ cup	1 cup	1¼ cups	1½ cups
butter or margarine (divided)	2 Tbsp	¼ cup	¼ cup + 2 Tbsp	½ cup	½ cup + 2 Tbsp	¾ cup
chicken broth	1⅓ cup	2½ cup	3⅓ cups	4¼ cups	5 cups	6 cups
canned mushrooms	4 oz.	8 oz.	12 oz.	16 oz.	20 oz.	24 oz.
all-purpose flour	1 Tbsp	2 Tbsp	3 Tbsp	¼ cup	¼ cup + 1 Tbsp	¼ cup + 2 Tbsp
salt	⅛ tsp	¼ tsp	¼ + ⅛ tsp	½ tsp	½ + ⅛ tsp	½ + ¼ tsp
white pepper	dash	⅛ tsp	⅛ tsp	¼ tsp	¼ tsp	¼ + ⅛ tsp
skim milk	½ cup	1 cup	1½ cups	2 cups	2½ cups	3 cups
dry white wine	¼ cup	½ cup	¾ cup	1 cup	1¼ cups	1½ cups
Swiss cheese, shredded	½ cup	1 cup	1½ cups	2 cups	2½ cups	3 cups

Thaw fish if frozen. In a saucepan sauté uncooked rice and onion in half of the butter or margarine for 5 minute or until rice is brown, stirring often. Stir in chicken broth. Bring to boiling, reduce heat. Cover and cook for 20 minutes. Drain mushrooms and add to rice mixture. Place rice mixture in greased co-op dishes. Top with fish fillets.

In a saucepan melt the remaining butter or margarine; stir in flour, salt, and pepper. Add milk; cook and stir with wire whisk until thickened and bubbly. Stir in wine. Pour sauce over fillets. Bake, uncovered, about 15 minutes at 400° F. Sprinkle with Swiss cheese. Bake 5 to 10 minutes more or until fish flakes easily with a fork.

Shrimp-and-Pasta Salad

Servings	6	12	18	24	30	36
frozen Rosetto Tortellini, 19-oz. package	1 pkg.	2 pkgs	3 pkgs	4 pkgs	5 pkgs	6 pkgs
peeled and deveined shrimp, cooked and chilled	12 oz. (¾ lb.)	24 oz. (1½ lb.)	36 oz. (2¼ lb.)	48 oz. (3 lb.)	60 oz. (3¾ lb.)	72 oz. (4½ lb.)
broccoli florets	1½ cups	3 cups	4½ cups	6 cups	7½ cups	9 cups
fresh pea pods	1 cup	2 cups	3 cups	4 cups	5 cups	6 cups
sweet red pepper, chopped	½ cup	1 cup	1½ cups	2 cups	2½ cups	3 cups
sweet onion, chopped	⅓ cup	⅔ cup	1 cup	1⅓ cups	1⅔ cups	2 cups
lettuce leaves, cleaned	6	12	18	24	30	36
clear Italian salad dressing	½ cup	1 cup	1½ cups	2 cups	2½ cups	3 cups

Place frozen tortellini in a colander; run cold water over pasta for 3 to 4 minutes or until thawed. (*Or*, place tortellini in a bowl. Pour cold water over tortellini and let stand about 10 minutes or until thawed.) Drain well.

In co-op dishes combine shrimp, broccoli, pea pods, red sweet pepper, and onion. Add tortellini; toss gently. Cover and refrigerate.

Place lettuce leaves in plastic bags for delivery. Measure clear Italian salad dressing into small glass jars.

Instructions for co-op families: Arrange salad on lettuce lined plates. Pass dressing to drizzle atop salads.

Thick and Hearty Clam Chowder

Servings	4	8	12	16	20	24
clam chowder, 15-oz. can	2 cans	4 cans	6 cans	8 cans	10 cans	12 cans
bacon slices, cooked, crumbled	2	4	6	8	10	12
beau monde seasoning	¼ tsp	¼ + ⅛ tsp	½ tsp	½ + ¼ tsp	1 tsp	1 ⅛ tsp
half & half cream	1 cup	2 cups	3 cups	4 cups	5 cups	6 cups
Ore-Ida Country-Style frozen hash browns, 26-oz. bag	¼ bag	½ bag	¾ bag	1 bag	1¼ bag	1½ bag
Ore-Ida frozen chopped onions	½ cup	1 cup	1½ cups	2 cups	2½ cups	3 cups
milk	½ cup	1 cup	1½ cups	2 cups	2½ cups	3 cups
chopped clams, 7-oz. can	1 can	2 cans	3 cans	4 cans	5 cans	6 cans

Combine cans of clam chowder, bacon, beau monde, and half & half in a large stock pot. Slowly warm (do not allow to boil). Combine hash brown potatoes and onions; prepare according to directions on hash brown package. When cooked, stir hash browns and onions into soup mixture. Add clams and milk; continue heating.

Instructions for co-op families: Reheat slowly; do not allow to boil.

Cream of Tomato Soup
Serve with sandwiches or homemade bread for a great tasting meal.

Servings (2 cups per serving)	4	8	12	16	20	24
diced tomatoes, 32-oz. cans	1 can	2 cans	3 cans	4 cans	5 cans	6 cans
chicken broth, undiluted	1 cup	2 cups	3 cups	4 cups	5 cups	6 cups
butter	1 Tbsp	2 Tbsp	3 Tbsp	¼ cup	¼ cup + 1 Tbsp	¼ cup + 2 Tbsp
sugar	1 Tbsp	2 Tbsp	3 Tbsp	¼ cup	¼ cup + 1 Tbsp	¼ cup + 2 Tbsp
chopped onion	2 Tbsp	¼ cup	¼ cup plus 2 Tbsp	½ cup	½ cup plus 2 Tbsp	¾ cup
baking soda	pinch	⅛ tsp	⅛ tsp	¼ tsp	¼ tsp	¼ + ⅛ tsp
half & half cream	2 cups (1 pint)	4 cups (1 quart)	6 cups	8 cups (2 quarts)	10 cups	12 cups (3 quarts)

Combine all ingredients, except the half & half cream, in a stock pot. Simmer one hour. Heat cream in a double boiler; add to the rest of the ingredients.
    Instructions for co-op families: Reheat slowly; do not allow to boil.

Johnny Cake
This sweet and tender corn bread is great with chili!

Servings	1 cake	2 cakes
egg	1	2
buttermilk	½ cup	1 cup
fat-free sour cream	½ cup	1 cup
baking soda	½ tsp	1 tsp
salt	½ tsp	1 tsp
yellow corn meal	1 cup	2 cups
unbleached flour	1 cup	2 cups
firmly packed brown sugar	¾ cup	1½ cups

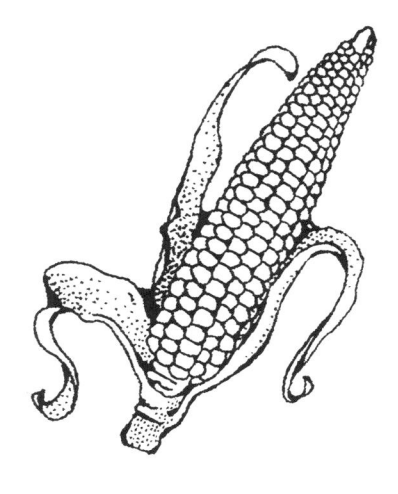

Beat the egg(s); stir in buttermilk and fat-free sour cream. In another bowl mix together the dry ingredients. Add the egg mixture to the dry ingredients and beat just until smooth (the dough will be stiff). Turn out into lightly greased 9" round cake pan(s). Bake at 450° F for 18 minutes or until a toothpick inserted into the middle comes out clean.

Aunt Babe's Onion Bread

	Makes 4 small loaves
yeast	2 pkg
warm water	¼ cup
fat free sour cream	1 cup
French onion soup mix	1.4 oz. package
baking soda	¼ tsp
sugar	2 Tbsp
butter, softened	2 Tbsp
eggs	4 (reserve one for egg wash)
all-purpose flour	6½-7 cups
sesame seeds	1 Tbsp

Sprinkle yeast over warm water in a small bowl. In a large bowl combine in the following order: sour cream, onion soup mix, baking soda, sugar, softened butter, 3 beaten eggs and one cup warm water. Stir in yeast mixture; mix until smooth. Add enough flour to form a stiff dough. Turn onto a floured surface and knead until smooth, about 10 minutes; place in a greased bowl and cover with a towel. Let rise until double in bulk, about 50 minutes. Punch down.

    Divide one quarter of the dough into three pieces. Roll each piece into a strip about 10 inches long. Braid the strips together and seal the ends. Repeat with the remaining dough. Place braids on a greased cookie sheet, cover and let rise about 30 minutes. Brush braids with the remaining beaten egg and sprinkle with sesame seeds. Bake at 350° F for 20 to 25 minutes or until golden brown. Cool on wire racks.

Louisiana Caviar
Use as a dip with tortilla chips.

Servings	4	8	12	16	20	24
black-eye peas, 15-oz. can	2 cans	4 cans	6 cans	8 cans	10 cans	12 cans
Italian dressing without oil	⅓ cup	⅔ cup	1 cup	1⅓ cups	1⅔ cups	2 cups
minced onions	⅔ cup	1⅓ cups	2 cups	2⅔ cups	3⅓ cups	4 cups
sweet green pepper, minced	1	2	3	4	5	6
canned chopped pimientos	2 ounces	4 ounces	6 ounces	8 ounces	10 ounces	12 ounces
diced canned green chili peppers	2 ounces	4 ounces	6 ounces	8 ounces	10 ounces	12 ounces
pickled jalapeños, diced	3	6	9	12	15	18
cloves garlic, minced	1	2	3	4	5	6

Combine all ingredients and marinate 8 hours or overnight.

Festive Rice

Servings	4	8	12	16	20	24
vegetable oil	2 tsp	1 Tbsp + 1 tsp	2 Tbsp	2 Tbsp + 2 tsp	3 Tbsp + 1 tsp	¼ cup
chopped sweet pepper	½ cup	1 cup	1½ cups	2 cups	2½ cups	3 cups
chopped onions	¼ cup	½ cup	¾ cup	1 cup	1¼ cups	1½ cups
chicken broth	1¼ cups	2½ cups	3¾ cups	5 cups	6¼ cups	7½ cups
salsa	½ cup	1 cup	1½ cups	2 cups	2½ cups	3 cups
frozen corn, thawed	¾ cup	1½ cups	2¼ cups	3 cups	3¾ cups	4½ cups
instant white rice, uncooked	1¼ cups	2½ cups	3¾ cups	5 cups	6¼ cups	7½ cups
canned black beans, drained	1 cup	2 cup	3 cups	4 cups	5 cups	6 cups
chopped fresh cilantro	1 Tbsp	2 Tbsp	3 Tbsp	¼ cup	¼ cup + 1 Tbsp	¼ cup + 2 Tbsp
garlic powder	⅛ tsp	¼ tsp	¼ + ⅛ tsp	½ tsp	½ + ⅛ tsp	½ + ¼ tsp
salt	¼ tsp	½ tsp	½ + ¼ tsp	1 tsp	1¼ tsp	½ Tbsp

Sauté pepper and onion in oil until onion is clear. Add broth, salsa, and corn; bring to a boil. Add rice, beans, cilantro, garlic powder and salt. Cover and let sit for 5 minutes or until all the liquid is absorbed.

Rice Pilaf

Servings	4	8	12	16	20	24
long grain rice, uncooked	¾ cup	1½ cup	2¼ cups	3 cups	3¾ cups	4½ cups
margarine	1 Tbsp	2 Tbsp	3 Tbsp	¼ cup	5 Tbsp	6 Tbsp
chopped onions	½ cup	1 cup	1½ cups	2 cups	2½ cups	3 cups
green bell peppers, chopped	¼ cup	½ cup	¾ cup	1 cup	1¼ cups	1½ cups
cloves of garlic, minced	1	2	3	4	5	6
instant chicken broth	½ Tbsp	2¼ tsp	1 Tbsp + a scant ½ tsp	1½ Tbsp	2 Tbsp	2 Tbsp + a scant tsp
black pepper	⅛ tsp	¼ tsp	¼ tsp	¼ + ⅛ tsp	½ tsp	½ tsp
water	1¾ cups	3¼ cups	4½ cups	6 cups	7½ cups	9 cups

Brown rice lightly in margarine stirring constantly. Add onions, green bell pepper, and garlic and cook until vegetables are tender. Stir in the instant chicken broth, black pepper and water. Bring to a boil, cover, and simmer until rice is cooked, about 20 minutes.

Mashed Potatoes Florentine

Servings	4	8	12	16	20	24
Ore-Ida Frozen Mashed Potatoes (22-ounce bag)	2⅔ cups (½ bag)	5⅓ cups (1 bag)	8 cups (1½ bags)	10⅔ cups (2 bags)	13⅓ cups (2½ bags)	16 cups (3 bags)
milk	1⅓ cups	2⅓ cups	3½ cups	4⅔ cups	5¾ cups	7 cups
butter or margarine, softened	2 Tbsp	¼ cup	6 Tbsp	½ cup	10 Tbsp	¾ cup
grated Parmesan cheese	2 Tbsp	¼ cup	6 Tbsp	½ cup	10 Tbsp	¾ cup
salt	½ tsp	1 tsp	½ Tbsp	2 tsp	2½ tsp	1 Tbsp
pepper	dash	⅛ tsp	⅛ tsp	¼ tsp	¼ tsp	¼ + ⅛ tsp
eggs	1	2	3	4	5	6
10-oz. pkg frozen chopped spinach, thawed and drained	½ pkg	1 pkg	1½ pkg	2 pkg	2½ pkg	3 pkg

Prepare mashed potatoes according to package directions using the quantity of milk indicated above.* Stir in margarine, Parmesan cheese, salt and pepper.

    In a small bowl beat eggs with a spoonful of potatoes. Turn the egg mixture into the rest of the potatoes and beat with an electric mixer for 2-3 minutes on medium speed. Squeeze small handfuls of spinach to remove as much water as possible. Break apart clumps with fork. Fold spinach into potato mixture. Spoon into greased casserole dishes. Bake for 35 minutes at 350° F.

Gourmet Mashed Potatoes

Servings	4	8	12	16	20	24
Ore-Ida Frozen Mashed Potatoes (22 ounce bag)	2⅔ cups (½ bag)	5⅓ cups (1 bag)	8 cups (1½ bags)	10⅔ cups (2 bags)	13⅓ cups (2½ bags)	16 cups (3 bags)
milk	1⅓ cups	2⅓ cups	3½ cups	4⅔ cups	5¾ cups	7 cups
sour cream**	¼ cup	½ cup	¾ cup	1 cup	1¼ cup	1½ cups

Top with one of the following, if desired:

green onions, sliced	¼ cup	½ cup	¾ cup	1 cup	1¼ cups	1½ cups
cheddar cheese, shredded	⅓ cup	⅔ cup	1 cup	1⅓ cups	1⅔ cups	2 cups
slivered almonds, toasted	2 Tbsp	¼ cup	¼ cup plus 2 Tbsp	½ cup	½ cup plus 2 Tbsp	¾ cup
bacon, cooked and crumbled	2 slices	4 slices	6 slices	8 slices	10 slices	12 slices

    Prepare mashed potatoes according to package directions using the quantity of milk indicated above.* Stir in sour cream. Sprinkle with one of the toppings (optional).

*If preparing more than 8 servings of potatoes, use the stove top method only.
**Use low-fat or fat-free sour cream to reduce the number of fat calories.

Creamy Au Gratin Potatoes

Servings	4	8	12	16	20	24
frozen Ore-Ida Chopped Onions	½ cup	1 cup	1½ cups	2 cups	2½ cups	3 cups
can (10½ ounce) condensed cream of celery or cream of mushroom soup	1 can	2 cans	3 cans	4 cans	5 cans	6 cans
cream cheese, cut in cubes	3 oz.	6 oz.	9 oz.	12 oz.	15 oz.	18 oz.
frozen Ore-Ida Southern Style Hash Browns*	4 cups	8 cups	12 cups	16 cups	20 cups	24 cups
cheddar cheese, shredded	⅓ cup	⅔ cup	1 cup	1⅓ cups	1⅔ cups	2 cups

Preheat oven to 400°F. Grease co-op dishes (use 1-quart or larger oven-proof casserole dish for 4 servings). Over medium heat cook frozen onions until tender. Stir in undiluted soup and cream cheese cubes: cook, stirring constantly, until smooth and hot. In co-op dishes alternately layer frozen potatoes and hot cream sauce ending with a sauce layer. Cover and bake 45 minutes or until sauce is bubbly and potatoes are tender. Remove from oven and sprinkle with shredded cheese.

May also be prepared with the following Ore-Ida products; Country Style Dinner Fries, Potatoes O'Brien, Cottage Fries.

Tangy Vegetable Potato Salad

Servings	4	8	12	16	20	24
small red potatoes	1 pound	2 pounds	3 pounds	4 pounds	5 pounds	6 pounds
clear Italian dressing	½ cup	1 cup	1½ cups	2 cups	2½ cups	3 cups
13-ounce can artichoke hearts, drained and halved	1 can	2 cans	3 cans	4 cans	5 cans	6 cans
small green pepper, sliced	1	2	3	4	5	6
cherry tomatoes, halved	6	12	18	24	30	36
green onions, sliced	1	2	3	4	5	6
pitted ripe olives, sliced	¼ cup	½ cup	¾ cup	1 cup	1¼ cups	1½ cups
snipped parsley	¼ cup	½ cup	¾ cup	1 cup	1¼ cups	1½ cups

Cook potatoes in boiling salted water just until tender — do not overcook. Drain well and cut into bite-sized pieces. In a large bowl gently mix together potatoes and Italian dressing. Add remaining ingredients and toss gently. Divide into co-op dishes; cover and refrigerate. Serve cold.

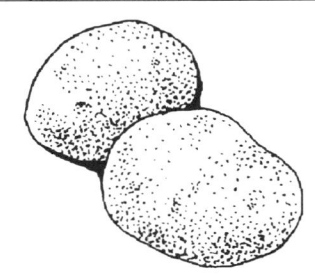

Green Beans with Almonds

Servings	4	8	12	16	20	24
frozen French-cut green beans	12 oz. (¾ lb.)	24 oz. (1 lb. 8 oz.)	36 oz. (2 lb. 4 oz.)	48 oz. (3 lb.)	60 oz. (3 lb. 12 oz.)	72 oz. (4 lb. 8 oz.)
slivered almonds	2 Tbsp	¼ cup	¼ cup + 2 Tbsp	½ cup	½ cup + 2 Tbsp	¾ cup
butter or margarine	½ Tbsp	1 Tbsp	1½ Tbsp	2 Tbsp	2½ Tbsp	3 Tbsp
lemon juice	1 tsp	2 tsp	1 Tbsp	1 Tbsp + 1 tsp	1 Tbsp + 2 tsp	2 Tbsp

Cook beans according to package instructions. Drain well. Place in co-op dishes.

Cook almonds in butter or margarine over medium heat until lightly browned. Remove from heat and add lemon juice. Spoon over green beans.

Asparagus with Egg Sauce

Servings	4	8	12	16	20	24
fresh asparagus spears	1 pound	2 pounds	3 pounds	4 pounds	5 pounds	6 pounds

Egg sauce

eggs, hard-cooked and peeled	2	4	6	8	10	12
butter or margarine, melted	2 Tbsp	¼ cup	¼ cup + 2 Tbsp	½ cup	½ cup + 2 Tbsp	¾ cup
lemon juice	2 Tbsp	¼ cup	¼ cup + 2 Tbsp	½ cup	½ cup + 2 Tbsp	¾ cup
fresh parsley, minced	1 Tbsp	2 Tbsp	3 Tbsp	¼ cup	¼ cup + 1 Tbsp	¼ cup + 2 Tbsp
salt	¼ tsp	½ tsp	½ + ¼ tsp	1 tsp	1¼ tsp	½ Tbsp
ground nutmeg	dash	⅛ tsp	⅛ tsp	¼ tsp	¼ tsp	¼ + ⅛ tsp

Prepare egg sauce: Combine sauce ingredients in a blender and mix until smooth. Pour into small containers for delivery to co-op families.

Wash asparagus and snap off woody ends. Cook, covered, in a small amount of water for about 10 minutes or until asparagus is just tender. (You may want to deliver the cleaned asparagus raw with instructions for cooking.)

Instructions for co-op families: Heat egg sauce in microwave for about one minute or until hot. Pour over hot asparagus.

Tomato and Avocado Salad

Servings	4	8	12	16	20	24
whole lettuce leaves	4	8	12	16	20	24
medium-sized tomatoes, sliced	4	8	12	16	20	24
avocados, peeled and sliced	1	2	3	4	5	6
Caesar salad dressing	⅓ cup	⅔ cup	1 cup	1⅓ cups	1⅔ cups	2 cups
hard-boiled eggs, chopped	1	2	3	4	5	6
black pepper (optional)						

Wash lettuce leaves and place in co-op dishes. Arrange tomato and avocado slices on lettuce leaves. Spoon on dressing. Sprinkle with chopped hard-boiled egg and black pepper, if desired.

Antipasto Salad

Servings	4	8	12	16	20	24
cherry tomatoes	1 pint	1 quart	1½ quarts	2 quarts	2½ quarts	3 quarts
sweet onion, thinly sliced	1	2	3	4	5	6
button mushrooms	1 cup	2 cup	3 cups	4 cups	5 cups	6 cups
pitted black olives	1 cup	2 cup	3 cups	4 cups	5 cups	6 cups
light Italian dressing	¼ cup	½ cup	¾ cup	1 cup	1¼ cups	1½ cups

Place tomatoes, onion slices, mushrooms, and black olives in co-op dishes. Top with Italian dressing. Chill.

Marinated Tomatoes

Servings	4	8	12	16	20	24
medium-sized tomatoes, sliced	4	8	12	16	20	24
olive oil	¼ cup	½ cup	¾ cup	1 cup	1¼ cups	1½ cups
red wine vinegar	2 Tbsp	¼ cup	¼ cup plus 2 Tbsp	½ cup	½ cup plus 2 Tbsp	¾ cup
salt	⅛ tsp	¼ tsp	¼ + ⅛ tsp	½ tsp	½ + ⅛ tsp	½ + ¼ tsp
red pepper sauce	3 drops	6 drops	9 drops	12 drops	15 drops	18 drops
cloves garlic, minced	2	4	6	8	10	12

Place tomato slices in co-op dishes. Mix remaining ingredients and pour over tomatoes. Serve chilled.

Coleslaw

Servings	4	8	12	16	20	24
sugar	2 Tbsp	¼ cup	¼ cup + 2 Tbsp	½ cup	½ cup + 2 Tbsp	¾ cup
vegetable oil	¼ cup	½ cup	¾ cup	1 cup	1¼ cups	1½ cups
cider vinegar	2 Tbsp	¼ cup	¼ cup + 2 Tbsp	½ cup	½ cup + 2 Tbsp	¾ cup
mayonnaise	2 Tbsp	¼ cup	¼ cup + 2 Tbsp	½ cup	½ cup + 2 Tbsp	¾ cup
celery seed	¼ tsp	½ tsp	½ + ¼ tsp	1 tsp	1¼ tsp	½ Tbsp
salt	¼ tsp	½ tsp	½ + ¼ tsp	1 tsp	1¼ tsp	½ Tbsp
black pepper	⅛ tsp	¼ tsp	¼ + ⅛ tsp	½ tsp	½ + ⅛ tsp	½ + ¼ tsp
green onions, sliced	1	2	3	4	5	6
green cabbage, shredded	½ medium	1 medium	1½ medium	2 medium	2½ medium	3 medium
large carrot, shredded	1	2	3	4	5	6

To make dressing combine sugar, oil, vinegar, mayonnaise, celery seed, salt and pepper in a blender and mix until smooth. Combine onion, cabbage and carrot in a large bowl. Stir in dressing. Refrigerate until ready to serve.

Waldorf Salad

Servings	4	8	12	16	20	24
seedless green grapes	½ cup	1 cup	1½ cups	2 cups	2½ cups	3 cups
diced red apple, unpeeled	½ cup	1 cup	1½ cups	2 cups	2½ cups	3 cups
sliced celery	½ cup	1 cup	1½ cups	2 cups	2½ cups	3 cups
chopped walnuts	¼ cup	½ cup	¾ cups	1 cup	1¼ cups	1½ cups
raisins	¼ cup	½ cup	¾ cups	1 cup	1¼ cups	1½ cups
whipping cream	¼ cup	½ cup	¾ cup	1 cup	1¼ cups	1½ cups
mayonnaise	¼ cup	½ cup	¾ cup	1 cup	1¼ cups	1½ cups
lemon juice	½ tsp	1 tsp	1½ tsp	2 tsp	2½ tsp	1 Tbsp
sugar	½ Tbsp	1 Tbsp	1½ Tbsp	2 Tbsp	2½ Tbsp	3 Tbsp

Combine fruit and nuts in a large bowl; toss. In a smaller bowl whip the cream; fold in mayonnaise, lemon juice and sugar. Stir whipped cream mixture into fruit and nuts. Chill before serving.

Stewed Apples

Servings	4	8	12	16	20	24
tart apples, peeled, cored, and cut into eighths	4	8	12	16	20	24
water	½ cup	1 cup	1½ cups	2 cups	2½ cups	3 cups
sugar	2 Tbsp	¼ cup	¼ cup plus 2 Tbsp	½ cup	½ cup plus 2 Tbsp	¾ cup
ground cinnamon (optional)	½ tsp	1 tsp	½ Tbsp	2 tsp	2½ tsp	1 Tbsp

In medium saucepan, combine apples and water. Cover and simmer until apples are tender, adding more water if needed. Stir in sugar and cinnamon. Serve warm.

Frozen Fruit Salad

Individual salads	1½ dozen	3 dozen	4½ dozen	6 dozen
canned crushed pineapple in juice (do not drain)	10 ounces	20 ounces	30 ounces	40 ounces
canned apricots, drained and cut up	8 ounces	16 ounces	24 ounces	32 ounces
medium bananas, sliced	1½	3	4½	6
10-oz. pkg frozen sliced strawberries*, thawed	1 pkg	2 pkg	3 pkg	4 pkg
sugar	¾ cup	1½ cups	2¼ cups	3 cups
water	½ cup	1 cup	1½ cups	2 cups
small marshmallows	½ cup	1 cup	1½ cups	2 cups

Combine fruit in a large bowl. Boil sugar and water for 5 minutes. Remove from heat. Add the marshmallows and stir until melted. When cool mix with fruit. Spoon into muffin cups lined with paper liners. Freeze. After frozen, remove from muffin tins and place in plastic freezer bags. Return to freezer until needed.
* *You can substitute two cups sliced fresh strawberries for each 10-ounce package of frozen strawberries.*

Fresh Fruit Salad

Allow one cup per serving. Use one or more fresh fruits that are in season. Your salad will be most appetizing if you select a variety of colors. Some of the fruits available in summer are watermelon, cantaloupe, honeydew melon, red and green grapes, strawberries, raspberries, blueberries, apricots, kiwi, peaches, and nectarines. In the winter the citrus fruits are in season — pink and red grapefruit, oranges, tangerines, and tangelos. If you use bananas, deliver them in the peel so that your co-op families can slice and add them at the last minute Canned pineapple is great with fresh fruit any time of the year. Golden Delicious apples won't change color if sliced.
Fresh Fruit Salad Dip: Mix an equal amount of flavored yogurt and frozen non-dairy whipped topping.
Company Fruit Salad: Mix a small package of instant vanilla pudding with the drained liquid of a 20-oz. can pineapple chunks and an 11-oz. can of mandarin oranges. Mix well. Pour over pineapple chunks, mandarin orange segments, and a mixture of other fruits such as grapes, strawberries and blueberries. *Makes 16 servings.*

Nutty Rum Ice Cream

Servings	6	12	18	24	30	36
blanched almonds, chopped	¼ cup	½ cup	¾ cup	1 cup	1¼ cups	1½ cups
flaked coconut	¼ cup	½ cup	¾ cup	1 cup	1¼ cups	1½ cups
softened vanilla ice cream	1 pint	1 quart	1 quart + 1 pint	½ gallon	½ gallon + 1 pint	½ gallon + 1 quart
rum extract	1 tsp	2 tsp	1 Tbsp	1 Tbsp + 1 tsp	1 Tbsp + 2 tsp	2 Tbsp
maraschino cherries, halved	4	6	9	12	15	18
paper muffin cups	6	12	18	24	30	36

Toast almonds and coconut: Heat oven to 325° F. Spread chopped almonds and coconut in a shallow baking pan. Bake for 10 minutes stirring occasionally. After the nut mixture has cooled crumble the coconut.

Stir together the softened vanilla ice cream and rum extract. Add half of the nut mixture to the ice cream and mix well. Spoon into paper muffin cups set into muffin tins.

Sprinkle remaining nut mixture onto the desserts. Top with maraschino cherry halves. Freeze until firm.

Heavenly Grapes

Servings	4	8	12	16	20	24
water	¼ cup	½ cup	¾ cup	1 cup	1¼ cups	1½ cups
egg	1	2	3	4	5	6
lemon juice	1½ Tbsp	3 Tbsp	¼ cup + ½ Tbsp	¼ cup + 2 Tbsp	¼ cup + 3½ Tbsp	½ cup + 1 Tbsp
sugar	¼ cup	½ cup	¾ cup	1 cup	1¼ cups	1½ cups
cornstarch	1 tsp	2 tsp	1 Tbsp	1 Tbsp + 1 tsp	1 Tbsp + 2 tsp	2 Tbsp
angel food cake slices	4	8	12	16	20	24
green grapes	2 cups	4 cups	6 cups	8 cups	10 cups	12 cups

Lemon sauce: In a bowl beat water, eggs and lemon juice together with a wire whisk. In a saucepan combine sugar and cornstarch. Gradually stir in beaten egg and lemon mixture. Cook and stir constantly over medium heat until thick and bubbly. Remove from heat. Put into containers for delivery.

Instructions for co-op families: Put cake slices in individual dessert dishes; top each slice with ½ cup grapes. Drizzle with lemon sauce.

Gratitude is the heart's memory. —FRENCH PROVERB

Appendix

Things to make your life easier

Here are the flyers and forms we promised you. We have included two different flyers, questionnaires for your first meeting, menu planning calendars, co-op evaluation sheets, shopping lists, recipe conversion cards in two sizes, and dinner tags. These should make forming, organizing and maintaining your co-op easy. Feel free to make copies for your own use.

In this Appendix you will find...

- **Flyers** - To find people interested in joining your co-op, distribute or post flyers in your neighborhood, church, workplace, or wherever people will see them. See pages 7 and 8.

- **Co-op Cooking Start-Up Questionnaire** - Use this questionnaire to determine if you and the people who have shown an interest in co-op cooking will make a compatible group. Read more about the questionnaire on pages 8 and 15.

- **Co-op Cooking Planning Calendar** - This six-week calendar will help you keep your menus varied and give you the information you need to supplement a meal if needed. Tips on using the calendar can be found on page 35.

- **Co-op Cooking Evaluation Sheet** - Follow-up meetings are important to keep your co-op running smoothly. The evaluation sheet is a non-threatening way to give your co-op a tune-up so that it gets better and better. You'll find further discussion of this subject on page 15.

- **Shopping List and Coupon Organizer** - Busy people appreciate streamlining, and that's what the organizer will help you do as you prepare to shop for your co-op meals.

- **Recipe Conversion Cards** - As you start cooking for more people, you'll want to record your recipes with ingredients multiplied to the proper amounts. We've provided two sizes of recipe cards for your convenience. Be sure to check out Chapter 4 for information on how to successfully multiply ingredients.

- **Dinner Tags** - You will frequently have last minute preparation instructions for the dinners you deliver. These tags are a convenient way to pass that information along to your co-op members. See page 39.

There is joy in giving... and receiving!

Are you tired of fishing around for dinner?

Would you like to plan and cook just one meal a week and receive delicious home-cooked meals the rest of the week?

If your answer is *yes*, then co-op cooking is for you!

For more information contact:

_____

at _____

Are you tired of fishing around for dinner?

Would you like to plan and cook just one meal a week and receive delicious home-cooked meals the rest of the week?

If your answer is *yes*, then co-op cooking is for you!

For more information contact:

_____

at _____

WHAT?! PIZZA FOR DINNER _AGAIN_?

Are you and your family tired of having fast food for dinner? Would you like to plan and cook just one meal a week and receive delicious home-cooked meals the rest of the week?

If your answer is *yes*, then co-op cooking is for you!

For more information contact:

_____

at _____

WHAT?! PIZZA FOR DINNER AGAIN?

Are you and your family tired of having fast food for dinner? Would you like to plan and cook just one meal a week and receive delicious home-cooked meals the rest of the week?

If your answer is *yes*, then co-op cooking is for you!

For more information contact:

_____

at _____

Co-op Cooking Start-Up Questionnaire

Name: _____ Phone: _____

Address: _____

1. What kind of meals do you prefer?
   - ☐ Fresh meals made daily.
   - ☐ Frozen meals exchanged weekly or monthly.
   - ☐ It doesn't matter to me.

2. What do you want your meals to consist of?
   - ☐ A complete, balanced meal that includes a meat or meat substitute, a side dish of salad, vegetables or fruit, and a carbohydrate such as bread, pasta, rice or potato.
   - ☐ Main dish only.
   - ☐ It doesn't matter to me.

3. Where do you prefer to make the meal exchange?
   - ☐ Neighborhood
   - ☐ Church
   - ☐ Work
   - ☐ Other _____

4. What are your family's dietary needs and preferences? (Check all that apply)
   - ☐ Meat and potatoes only
   - ☐ Reasonable and varied diet
   - ☐ Low fat/ low cholesterol
   - ☐ Vegetarian
   - ☐ Kosher
   - ☐ Food allergies (specify) _____
   - ☐ Other (specify) _____

5. What is your family size?
   - ☐ Single
   - ☐ Couple
   - ☐ _____ Adults (including teenagers) and _____ young children

6. How many servings do you usually cook for your family? _____

7. Are there any foods that your family will not eat? _____

8. What is your family's all-time favorite meal? _____

9. Which day of the week would be most convenient for you to cook? _____

10. What is the earliest time of day you are likely to eat dinner? _____

11. I agree to read the chapter on food safety in *Homemade To Go* by Bower and Wells, and to follow the recommendations given. (yes / no)

Co-op Cooking Start-Up Questionnaire

Name: _____ Phone: _____

Address: _____

1. What kind of meals do you prefer?
   - ☐ Fresh meals made daily.
   - ☐ Frozen meals exchanged weekly or monthly.
   - ☐ It doesn't matter to me.

2. What do you want your meals to consist of?
   - ☐ A complete, balanced meal that includes a meat or meat substitute, a side dish of salad, vegetables or fruit, and a carbohydrate such as bread, pasta, rice or potato.
   - ☐ Main dish only.
   - ☐ It doesn't matter to me.

3. Where do you prefer to make the meal exchange?
   - ☐ Neighborhood
   - ☐ Church
   - ☐ Work
   - ☐ Other _____

4. What are your family's dietary needs and preferences? (Check all that apply)
   - ☐ Meat and potatoes only
   - ☐ Reasonable and varied diet
   - ☐ Low fat/ low cholesterol
   - ☐ Vegetarian
   - ☐ Kosher
   - ☐ Food allergies (specify) _____
   - ☐ Other (specify) _____

5. What is your family size?
   - ☐ Single
   - ☐ Couple
   - ☐ ____ Adults (including teenagers) and ____ young children

6. How many servings do you usually cook for your family? _____

7. Are there any foods that your family will not eat? _____

8. What is your family's all-time favorite meal? _____

9. Which day of the week would be most convenient for you to cook? _____

10. What is the earliest time of day you are likely to eat dinner? _____

11. I agree to read the chapter on food safety in *Homemade To Go* by Bower and Wells, and to follow the recommendations given. (yes / no)

Co-op Cooking Start-Up Questionnaire

Name: _____ Phone: _____

Address: _____

1. What kind of meals do you prefer?
   - ☐ Fresh meals made daily.
   - ☐ Frozen meals exchanged weekly or monthly.
   - ☐ It doesn't matter to me.

2. What do you want your meals to consist of?
   - ☐ A complete, balanced meal that includes a meat or meat substitute, a side dish of salad, vegetables or fruit, and a carbohydrate such as bread, pasta, rice or potato.
   - ☐ Main dish only.
   - ☐ It doesn't matter to me.

3. Where do you prefer to make the meal exchange?
   - ☐ Neighborhood
   - ☐ Church
   - ☐ Work
   - ☐ Other _____

4. What are your family's dietary needs and preferences? (Check all that apply)
   - ☐ Meat and potatoes only
   - ☐ Reasonable and varied diet
   - ☐ Low fat/ low cholesterol
   - ☐ Vegetarian
   - ☐ Kosher
   - ☐ Food allergies (specify) _____
   - ☐ Other (specify) _____

5. What is your family size?
   - ☐ Single
   - ☐ Couple
   - ☐ ____ Adults (including teenagers) and ____ young children

6. How many servings do you usually cook for your family? _____

7. Are there any foods that your family will not eat? _____

8. What is your family's all-time favorite meal? _____

9. Which day of the week would be most convenient for you to cook? _____

10. What is the earliest time of day you are likely to eat dinner? _____

11. I agree to read the chapter on food safety in *Homemade To Go* by Bower and Wells, and to follow the recommendations given. (yes / no)

Co-op Cooking Planning Calendar

For the time period _____ to _____

Monday	Tuesday	Wednesday	Thursday	Friday

Co-op Cooking Planning Calendar

For the time period _____ to _____

Monday	Tuesday	Wednesday	Thursday	Friday

Co-op Cooking Planning Calendar

For the time period _____ to _____

Monday	Tuesday	Wednesday	Thursday	Friday

Co-op Cooking Evaluation Sheet

1. List your favorite meals from the last few weeks:

2. What <u>new</u> dish(es) did you especially enjoy?

3. What meal(s) did your children enjoy the most?

4. What kind of meal(s) would you like to have <u>more</u> often (ethnic, grilled, low-fat, seafood, etc.)

5. What kind of meal(s) would you like to have <u>less</u> often?

6. Are there side dish(es) that you would like to have <u>more</u> often (rice, potatoes, salad, fruit, etc.)?

7. Are there side dish(es) that you would like to have <u>less</u> often?

8. Do your meals arrive on time? Or, are they ready to be picked up when you need them?

9. Does the food seem fresh?

10. Do you receive the right amount of food for your family? Too much? Too little?

11. Are you able to keep within the budget?

12. On a scale of 1 to 10, how is the co-op meeting your family's needs?

13. In what way could the co-op better meet your needs?

14. Other comments or suggestions:

Co-op Cooking Evaluation Sheet

1. List your favorite meals from the last few weeks:

2. What new dish(es) did you especially enjoy?

3. What meal(s) did your children enjoy the most?

4. What kind of meal(s) would you like to have more often (ethnic, grilled, low-fat, seafood, etc.)

5. What kind of meal(s) would you like to have less often?

6. Are there side dish(es) that you would like to have more often (rice, potatoes, salad, fruit, etc.)?

7. Are there side dish(es) that you would like to have less often?

8. Do your meals arrive on time? Or, are they ready to be picked up when you need them?

9. Does the food seem fresh?

10. Do you receive the right amount of food for your family? Too much? Too little?

11. Are you able to keep within the budget?

12. On a scale of 1 to 10, how is the co-op meeting your family's needs?

13. In what way could the co-op better meet your needs?

14. Other comments or suggestions:

Co-op Cooking Evaluation Sheet

1. List your favorite meals from the last few weeks:

2. What <u>new</u> dish(es) did you especially enjoy?

3. What meal(s) did your children enjoy the most?

4. What kind of meal(s) would you like to have <u>more</u> often (ethnic, grilled, low-fat, seafood, etc.)

5. What kind of meal(s) would you like to have <u>less</u> often?

6. Are there side dish(es) that you would like to have <u>more</u> often (rice, potatoes, salad, fruit, etc.)?

7. Are there side dish(es) that you would like to have <u>less</u> often?

8. Do your meals arrive on time? Or, are they ready to be picked up when you need them?

9. Does the food seem fresh?

10. Do you receive the right amount of food for your family? Too much? Too little?

11. Are you able to keep within the budget?

12. On a scale of 1 to 10, how is the co-op meeting your family's needs?

13. In what way could the co-op better meet your needs?

14. Other comments or suggestions:

Shopping List for ____ (date)

Fruits and Vegetables (Bananas, apples, onions, potatoes, tomatoes, lettuce)
- ☐ _____
- ☐ _____
- ☐ _____
- ☐ _____

Bakery and Deli (Bread, rolls, lunch meat)
- ☐ _____
- ☐ _____
- ☐ _____
- ☐ _____

Meat, poultry and fish
- ☐ _____
- ☐ _____
- ☐ _____
- ☐ _____

Dairy (Milk, eggs, butter, margarine, yogurt, cheese)
- ☐ _____
- ☐ _____
- ☐ _____
- ☐ _____

Frozen Food (Juice, vegetables, ice cream)
- ☐ _____
- ☐ _____
- ☐ _____
- ☐ _____

Staples (Peanut butter, jelly, catsup, salad dressing)
- ☐ _____
- ☐ _____
- ☐ _____

Baking Products (Flour, sugar, salt, oil, spices)
- ☐ _____
- ☐ _____
- ☐ _____

Canned Goods (Soup, tomato sauce, mushrooms)
- ☐ _____
- ☐ _____
- ☐ _____

Household (Toilet paper, laundry detergent, soap, light bulbs, plastic bags)
- ☐ _____
- ☐ _____
- ☐ _____

Health/ Beauty (Toothpaste, deodorant, shampoo)
- ☐ _____
- ☐ _____
- ☐ _____

Other (Pet food, soft drinks, chips, batteries, greeting cards)
- ☐ _____
- ☐ _____
- ☐ _____

(Turn page over for directions)

Coupons

Directions

1. Create coupon pocket following diagrams below.

2. Write down what coupons you have when you put them in the pocket. If you have a coupon for an item on your list, put a check mark in the box next to it.

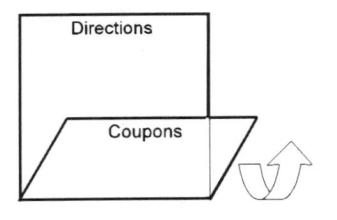

Fold bottom up along dotted line as shown.

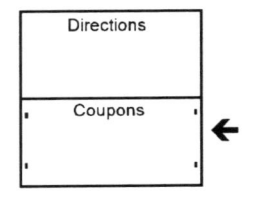

Staple or tape sides.
Insert coupons in pocket.

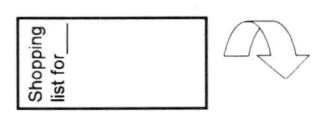

Fold top down along dotted line.
Your shopping list is ready to use.

Shopping List for _____ (date)

Fruits and Vegetables (Bananas, apples, onions, potatoes, tomatoes, lettuce)
- ☐ _____
- ☐ _____
- ☐ _____
- ☐ _____
- ☐ _____
- ☐ _____
- ☐ _____
- ☐ _____

Bakery and Deli (Bread, rolls, lunch meat)
- ☐ _____
- ☐ _____
- ☐ _____
- ☐ _____
- ☐ _____
- ☐ _____
- ☐ _____
- ☐ _____

Meat, poultry and fish
- ☐ _____
- ☐ _____
- ☐ _____
- ☐ _____
- ☐ _____
- ☐ _____
- ☐ _____
- ☐ _____

Dairy (Milk, eggs, butter, margarine, yogurt, cheese)
- ☐ _____
- ☐ _____
- ☐ _____
- ☐ _____
- ☐ _____
- ☐ _____
- ☐ _____
- ☐ _____

Frozen Food (Juice, vegetables, ice cream)
- ☐ _____
- ☐ _____
- ☐ _____
- ☐ _____
- ☐ _____
- ☐ _____
- ☐ _____
- ☐ _____

Staples (Peanut butter, jelly, catsup, salad dressing)
- ☐ _____
- ☐ _____
- ☐ _____
- ☐ _____

Baking Products (Flour, sugar, salt, oil, spices)
- ☐ _____
- ☐ _____
- ☐ _____
- ☐ _____

Canned Goods (Soup, tomato sauce, mushrooms)
- ☐ _____
- ☐ _____
- ☐ _____
- ☐ _____

Household (Toilet paper, laundry detergent, soap, light bulbs, plastic bags)
- ☐ _____
- ☐ _____
- ☐ _____
- ☐ _____

Health/ Beauty (Toothpaste, deodorant, shampoo)
- ☐ _____
- ☐ _____
- ☐ _____
- ☐ _____

Other (Pet food, soft drinks, chips, batteries, greeting cards)
- ☐ _____
- ☐ _____
- ☐ _____
- ☐ _____

(Turn page over for directions)

Coupons

Directions

1. Create coupon pocket following diagrams below.

2. Write down what coupons you have when you put them in the pocket. If you have a coupon for an item on your list, put a check mark in the box next to it.

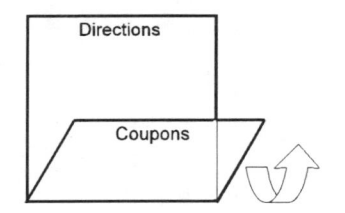

Fold bottom up along dotted line as shown.

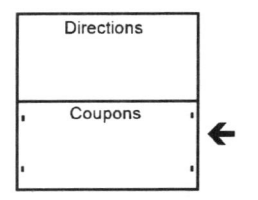

Staple or tape sides. Insert coupons in pocket.

Fold top down along dotted line. Your shopping list is ready to use.

Shopping List for (date) ____

Fruits and Vegetables (Bananas, apples, onions, potatoes, tomatoes, lettuce)

☐ _____ ☐ _____
☐ _____ ☐ _____
☐ _____ ☐ _____
☐ _____ ☐ _____
☐ _____ ☐ _____

Bakery and Deli (Bread, rolls, lunch meat)

☐ _____ ☐ _____
☐ _____ ☐ _____
☐ _____ ☐ _____
☐ _____ ☐ _____
☐ _____ ☐ _____

Meat, poultry and fish

☐ _____ ☐ _____
☐ _____ ☐ _____
☐ _____ ☐ _____
☐ _____ ☐ _____
☐ _____ ☐ _____

Dairy (Milk, eggs, butter, margarine, yogurt, cheese)

☐ _____ ☐ _____
☐ _____ ☐ _____
☐ _____ ☐ _____
☐ _____ ☐ _____
☐ _____ ☐ _____

Frozen Food (Juice, vegetables, ice cream)

☐ _____ ☐ _____
☐ _____ ☐ _____
☐ _____ ☐ _____
☐ _____ ☐ _____
☐ _____ ☐ _____

Staples (Peanut butter, jelly, catsup, salad dressing)

☐ _____ ☐ _____
☐ _____ ☐ _____
☐ _____ ☐ _____
☐ _____ ☐ _____
☐ _____ ☐ _____

Baking Products (Flour, sugar, salt, oil, spices)

☐ _____ ☐ _____
☐ _____ ☐ _____
☐ _____ ☐ _____
☐ _____ ☐ _____
☐ _____ ☐ _____

Canned Goods (Soup, tomato sauce, mushrooms)

☐ _____ ☐ _____
☐ _____ ☐ _____
☐ _____ ☐ _____
☐ _____ ☐ _____
☐ _____ ☐ _____

Household (Toilet paper, laundry detergent, soap, light bulbs, plastic bags)

☐ _____ ☐ _____
☐ _____ ☐ _____
☐ _____ ☐ _____
☐ _____ ☐ _____
☐ _____ ☐ _____

Health/ Beauty (Toothpaste, deodorant, shampoo)

☐ _____ ☐ _____
☐ _____ ☐ _____
☐ _____ ☐ _____
☐ _____ ☐ _____
☐ _____ ☐ _____

Other (Pet food, soft drinks, chips, batteries, greeting cards)

☐ _____ ☐ _____
☐ _____ ☐ _____
☐ _____ ☐ _____
☐ _____ ☐ _____
☐ _____ ☐ _____

(Turn page over for directions)

Coupons

_____ _____ _____
_____ _____ _____
_____ _____ _____
_____ _____ _____
_____ _____ _____
_____ _____ _____

Directions

1. Create coupon pocket following diagrams below.

2. Write down what coupons you have when you put them in the pocket. If you have a coupon for an item on your list, put a check mark in the box next to it.

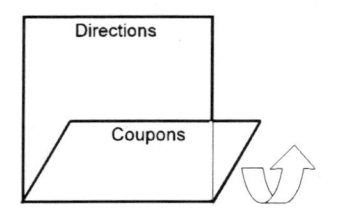

Fold bottom up along dotted line as shown.

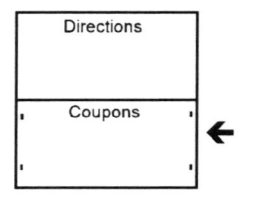

Staple or tape sides. Insert coupons in pocket.

Fold top down along dotted line. Your shopping list is ready to use.

Recipe for _____

Source of original recipe _____

Original makes _____ servings | Quantity for _____ servings | Ingredients

(blank lines)

Directions:

Recipe for _____

Source of original recipe _____

Original makes _____ servings | Quantity for _____ servings | Ingredients

(blank lines)

Directions:

Recipe for _____

Source of original recipe _____

Original makes ___ servings	Quantity for ___ servings	Ingredients

Directions:

Recipe for _____

Source of original recipe _____

Original makes ___ servings	Quantity for ___ servings	Ingredients

Directions:

Recipe for _____

Source of original recipe _____

Original makes ___ servings	Quantity for ___ servings	Ingredients
_____	_____	_____
_____	_____	_____
_____	_____	_____
_____	_____	_____
_____	_____	_____
_____	_____	_____
_____	_____	_____
_____	_____	_____
_____	_____	_____
_____	_____	_____
_____	_____	_____
_____	_____	_____
_____	_____	_____

Directions:

Recipe for _____

Source of original recipe _____

Original makes ___ servings	Quantity for ___ servings	Ingredients
_____	_____	_____
_____	_____	_____
_____	_____	_____
_____	_____	_____
_____	_____	_____
_____	_____	_____
_____	_____	_____
_____	_____	_____
_____	_____	_____
_____	_____	_____
_____	_____	_____
_____	_____	_____
_____	_____	_____

Directions:

Recipe Conversion Cards

Recipe for

Source of original recipe

Original makes ____ servings   Quantity for ____ servings   Ingredients

Turn over for directions.

Recipe for

Source of original recipe

Original makes ____ servings   Quantity for ____ servings   Ingredients

Turn over for directions.

Recipe for

Source of original recipe

Original makes ____ servings   Quantity for ____ servings   Ingredients

Turn over for directions.

Recipe for

Source of original recipe

Original makes ____ servings   Quantity for ____ servings   Ingredients

Turn over for directions.

Recipe Conversion Cards

Recipe for _____

Source of original recipe _____

Original makes ___ servings

Quantity for ___ servings

Ingredients

_____
_____
_____
_____
_____
_____
_____
_____
_____

Turn over for directions.

Recipe for _____

Source of original recipe _____

Original makes ___ servings

Quantity for ___ servings

Ingredients

_____
_____
_____
_____
_____
_____
_____
_____
_____

Turn over for directions.

Recipe for _____

Source of original recipe _____

Original makes ___ servings

Quantity for ___ servings

Ingredients

_____
_____
_____
_____
_____
_____
_____
_____
_____

Turn over for directions.

Recipe for _____

Source of original recipe _____

Original makes ___ servings

Quantity for ___ servings

Ingredients

_____
_____
_____
_____
_____
_____
_____
_____
_____

Turn over for directions.

Recipe Conversion Cards

Recipe for _____

Source of original recipe _____

Original makes ___ servings

Quantity for ___ servings

Ingredients

_____
_____
_____
_____
_____
_____
_____
_____
_____

Turn over for directions.

Recipe for _____

Source of original recipe _____

Original makes ___ servings

Quantity for ___ servings

Ingredients

_____
_____
_____
_____
_____
_____
_____
_____
_____

Turn over for directions.

Recipe for _____

Source of original recipe _____

Original makes ___ servings

Quantity for ___ servings

Ingredients

_____
_____
_____
_____
_____
_____
_____
_____
_____

Turn over for directions.

Recipe for _____

Source of original recipe _____

Original makes ___ servings

Quantity for ___ servings

Ingredients

_____
_____
_____
_____
_____
_____
_____
_____
_____

Turn over for directions.

Dinner Tags

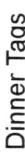

Tonight's Menu

_____
_____
_____

Preparation & serving instructions:

_____
_____
_____
_____
_____
_____

Tonight's Menu

_____
_____
_____

Preparation & serving instructions:

_____
_____
_____
_____
_____
_____

Tonight's Menu

_____
_____
_____

Preparation & serving instructions:

_____
_____
_____
_____
_____
_____

Tonight's Menu

_____
_____
_____

Preparation & serving instructions:

_____
_____
_____
_____
_____
_____

Tonight's Menu

_____
_____
_____

Preparation & serving instructions:

_____
_____
_____
_____
_____
_____

Tonight's Menu

_____
_____
_____

Preparation & serving instructions:

_____
_____
_____
_____
_____
_____

Dinner Tags

Tonight's Menu

_____
_____
_____

Preparation & serving instructions:

_____
_____
_____
_____
_____

Tonight's Menu

_____
_____
_____

Preparation & serving instructions:

_____
_____
_____
_____
_____

Tonight's Menu

_____
_____
_____

Preparation & serving instructions:

_____
_____
_____
_____
_____
_____

Tonight's Menu

_____
_____
_____

Preparation & serving instructions:

_____
_____
_____
_____
_____
_____

Tonight's Menu

_____
_____
_____

Preparation & serving instructions:

_____
_____
_____
_____
_____

Tonight's Menu

_____
_____
_____

Preparation & serving instructions:

_____
_____
_____
_____
_____

Tonight's Menu

_____
_____
_____

Preparation & serving instructions:

_____
_____
_____
_____
_____
_____

Tonight's Menu

_____
_____
_____

Preparation & serving instructions:

_____
_____
_____
_____
_____
_____

Tonight's Menu

_____
_____
_____

Preparation & serving instructions:

_____
_____
_____
_____
_____
_____

Tonight's Menu

_____
_____
_____

Preparation & serving instructions:

_____
_____
_____
_____
_____
_____

Tonight's Menu

_____
_____
_____

Preparation & serving instructions:

_____
_____
_____
_____
_____
_____

Tonight's Menu

_____
_____
_____

Preparation & serving instructions:

_____
_____
_____
_____
_____
_____

Dinner Tags

General Index

A

Advantages of co-op cooking 3
Advertise your co-op 7, 8, 66
Advice
  asking for 17
Allergies 6, 32
Amount of food to fix 13
Appetite 2, 6

B

Bacterial growth and temperature 30
Baked goods
  multiplying recipes for 20
Beef
  cooking temperatures 29
  thawing 31
Best dishes to serve 26
Bleach, as a disinfectant 28
Budget 14
Buying in bulk 26

C

Calendars 12, 25, 35, 66. *See also* Appendix
Chicken
  cooking temperatures 29
  thawing 31
Children
  meal planning and 36
Church (or synagogue) 7
  forming groups at 6
Co-op Cooking Evaluation Sheet 15
Co-op Cooking Start-Up Questionnaire 9, 15. *See also* Appendix
Cold foods cold, keeping 28, 30
Cold water, thawing food in 31
Color of food 34
Community
  creating a sense of 3
Company 15, 17
Compliments 17
Computer programs 22
Containers 7, 13, 25
  delivering 17
Cooking
  equipment 22
  for a crowd. *See* Chapter 4
  lack of ability 4
  tips for co-ops 25
Cooking co-op
  advantages 3
  defined 2, 12
  disadvantages 3
  how it all got started 2
  ingredients of successful 2
  neighborhood 2
  notes about my 17
  reasons to start 3
  stopping temporarily 14
  ways to build a successful 17
Cooling cooked food 31
Cooperative Extension Service 32
Counter tops, washing 28
Coupon Organizer 66. *See also* Appendix
Cutting boards 29

D

Delivering food 6, 7, 12, 17
  how to 13
  when to 13
Dietary needs and preferences 6
Dinner Tags 39, 66. *See also* Appendix
Dinner-time stress 3
Disadvantages of co-op cooking 3
Dishes 13
  delivering to next cook 14
Do you eat together? 12

E

Early American meals to go 14
Emergencies 15
Emergency meals 15
Equivalents 22, 24
Evaluation Sheet 15
Exchanging meals 14
Extension Service, Cooperative 32

F

Family
  appetite 6
  mealtimes 13
  size 6, 14
Fast food 3
Feedback on a meal 17

Fish
  amount to prepare 23
  thawing 31
Flavor of food, combining 35
Flops 17
Flyers 8, 66. *See also* Appendix
Food
  allergies 6, 32
  amount to fix 13
  cooling 31
  safety 15. *See also* Chapter 5
  temperature and time of year 35
  thawing 31
  to keep on hand 15
Food and Drug Administration 32
Food Guide Pyramid 34
Food poisoning 27, 28
Food-borne illness 27
Forming your co-op. *See* Chapter 2
Forms and flyers. *See* Appendix, pages 63-114
Freezer
  investing in 26
  temperatures 30
Freezing your meals 7
  disadvantages of 7
Frozen food, cooking 29

G

Getting started. *See* Chapter 3
Goose or gosling
  amount to prepare 23
  thawing 31

H

Ham
  cooking temperatures 29
  thawing 31
Handy cooking equipment to own 22
Health problems 7
Holidays 17
Honest, being 17
Hot foods hot, keeping 28, 29
Household pests, controlling 28
How does a cooking co-op work? 12
How it all got started 2
How much food to prepare 23
How much time does it take? 12

I

Information on food safety 32
Ingredients
   multiplying 20

K

Kid factor 36
Kitchen, keeping it clean and safe 28
Kosher diet 6

L

Lamb
   cooking temperatures 29
   thawing 31
Leftovers, reheating 29
Lifestyles 2, 6, 7
Low fat / low cholesterol diet 6

M

Meals
   delivering 2, 17
   exchanging 14
Meat
   amount to prepare 23
   cooking temperatures 29
   thawing 31
Meat and Poultry Hotline 32
Meeting 8
Menu ideas 36
Menus 3
Microwave, thawing food in 31
Mistakes 17
Money, saving 3
Multiplying
   all other ingredients 21
   recipes 20
   seasonings in soups, stews, etc. 20
Murphy's Law 3

N

Needs and preferences 6
Notes about my co-op 17
Nutrition 34

P

Planning calendars 35, 66. *See also* Appendix

Planning your meals. *See* Chapter 6
Portions 13
Poultry
   amount to prepare 23
   cooking temperatures 29
   thawing 31
Problems
   avoiding 15
   dealing with 17

Q

Quantity, cooking in. *See* Chapter 4 and Chapter 7
Questionnaire, Start-Up
   8, 9, 15, 66. *See also* Appendix

R

Recipe computer programs 22
Recipe Conversion Cards
   22, 66. *See also* Appendix
Recipes. *See* Chapter 7 and Recipe Index, page 117
Recipes, multiplying. *See* Chapter 4
Refrigerator temperatures 30
Refrigerator, thawing food in 31
Reheating food 29
Rolls and bread, amount to fix 23
Rules for cooking safely 28
Rules for multiplying ingredients in recipes 20

S

Safe food storage 28
Salad, delivering 25
Salads and vegetables, amount to prepare 23
Sales 26
Sample menus 36
Scheduling menus 12
Seasonings
   and the "kid factor" 36
   multiplying 20
"Sell by" date 31
Senior citizens 7
Sensitive, being 17
Servings 6
Shopping 3, 30, 31
Shopping List 66. *See also* Appendix

Sponges, to sterilize 29
Spoon-lickers 15
Start-Up Questionnaire
   8, 9, 15, 66. *See also* Appendix
Stir-fry, tip for preparing 25
Substitutes and equivalents 24
Successful cooking co-op 2, 6, 7
   ways to build 17
Support and special interest groups 7
Surfaces, to disinfect 28

T

Take it easy 25
Tastes in food 6
Temperature, and bacterial growth 30
Texture of food 35
Thawing meat and poultry 31
Time it takes to cook a co-op meal 12
Tips
   for a great first meeting 7
   to make cooking easier 25
Turkey
   cooking temperatures 29
   thawing 31
Types of co-ops 7

U

U.S. Department of Agriculture
   as a source of information 32
   Food Guide Pyramid 34
"Use by" dates 31
Using Recipe Conversion Cards 22

V

Vacation 14
Veal
   cooking temperatures 29
   thawing 31
Vegetarian diet 6

W

What do you fix? 12
What is co-op cooking? 2
Where to find co-op members 7
Work as a place to find co-op members 7

Recipe Index

A

Antipasto Salad 59
Apples, stewed 61
Asian Beef Kabobs 44
Asparagus with Egg Sauce 59
Aunt Babe's Onion Bread 54

B

Barbecue Beef Cups 43
Barbecue Beef Tri-Tip 41
Beans, Green with Almonds
   Green Beans with Almonds 58
Beef
   Asian Beef Kabobs 44
   Barbecue Beef Tri-Tip 41
   Beef Vegetable Stir-Fry 41
   Crock-Pot Roast 43
   ground
      Barbecue Beef Cups 43
      Beef and Cabbage Braid 42
      Spaghetti Sauce with Meat 40
      Steak and Cheese Braid 42
Beef and Cabbage Braid 42
Beef Vegetable Stir-Fry 41
Black-eye peas
   Louisiana Caviar 54
Braids
   directions for shaping 42
Breads
   Aunt Babe's Onion Bread 54
   Cheesy French Bread 40
   Johnny Cake 53
   main dish
      Barbecue Beef Cups 43
      Beef and Cabbage Braid 42
      Ham and Cheese Braid 42
      Reuben Braid 42
      Steak and Cheese Braid 42
Broiled Salmon Steaks 51

C

Cheese Ravioli with Marinara 50
Cheesy French Bread 40
Chicken
   Chicken Enchiladas 47
   Chicken Parmigiana 49
   Chicken Pasta Medley 48
   Chicken Pie 48
   Moroccan Sandwiches 49
Chicken Enchiladas 47
Chicken Parmigiana 49
Chicken Pasta Medley 48
Chicken Pie 48
Coleslaw 60
Company Fruit Salad 61
Corn bread
   Johnny Cake 53
Cream of Tomato Soup 53
Creamy Au Gratin Potatoes 57
Crock-Pot Roast 43

D

Desserts
   Company Fruit Salad 61
   Frozen Fruit Salad 61
   Heavenly Grapes 62
   Nutty Rum Ice Cream 62
Dips
   Fresh Fruit Salad Dip 61
   Louisiana Caviar 54
Directions for shaping braids 42

F

Festive Rice 55
Fish Fillets on Rice 51
Fresh Fruit Salad 61
Fresh Fruit Salad Dip 61
Frozen Fruit Salad 61
Fruit
   Company Fruit Salad 61
   Fresh Fruit Salad 61
   Frozen Fruit Salad 61
   Heavenly Grapes 62
   Stewed Apples 61
   Waldorf Salad 60

G

Gourmet Mashed Potatoes 56
Green Beans with Almonds 58

H

Ham and Cheese Braid 42
Hawaiian Sausage Stir-Fry 45
Heavenly Grapes 62

I

Italian Pasta Bake 44

J

Johnny Cake 53

L

Louisiana Caviar 54

M

Marinated Tomatoes 59
Mashed Potatoes Florentine 56
Moroccan Sandwiches 49

N

Nutty Rum Ice Cream 62

O

Ore-Ida products, recipes using
   frozen chopped onions
      Creamy Au Gratin Potatoes 57
      Thick and Hearty Clam Chowder 52
   frozen potatoes
      Creamy Au Gratin Potatoes 57
      Gourmet Mashed Potatoes 56
      Mashed Potatoes Florentine 56
      Thick and Hearty Clam Chowder 52

P

Pasta
   Cheese Ravioli with Marinara 50
   Chicken Pasta Medley 48
   Italian Pasta Bake 44
   Shrimp-and-Pasta Salad 52
   Spaghetti Sauce with Meat 40
Pastrami
   Reuben Braid 42
Pork
   Ham and Cheese Braid 42
   Pork Chop and Potato Casserole 47
   Pork Loin Roll-Ups 46
   South of the Border Pork Tenderloin 46

Spicy Skillet Pork 45
Pork Chop and Potato Casserole 47
Pork Loin Roll-Ups 46
Potato
    Creamy Au Gratin Potatoes 57
    Gourmet Mashed Potatoes 56
    Mashed Potatoes Florentine 56
    Pork Chop and Potato Casserole 47
    Tangy Vegetable Potato Salad 57
Potatoes
    Crock-Pot Roast 43

R

Reuben Braid 42
Rice
    Festive Rice 55
    Fish Fillets on Rice 51
    Rice Pilaf 55
Rice Pilaf 55
Rosetto products, recipes using
    Cheese Ravioli with Marinara 50
    Shrimp-and-Pasta Salad 52

S

Salads
    Antipasto Salad 59
    Coleslaw 60
    Company Fruit Salad 61
    Fresh Fruit Salad 61
    Frozen Fruit Salad 61
    Marinated Tomatoes 59
    Shrimp-and-Pasta Salad 52
    Tangy Vegetable Potato Salad 57
    Tomato and Avocado Salad 59
    Waldorf Salad 60
Sausage
    Hawaiian Sausage Stir-Fry 45
    Italian
        Italian Pasta Bake 44
        Spaghetti Sauce with Meat 40
Seafood
    Broiled Salmon Steaks 51
    Fish Fillets on Rice 51
    Shrimp-and-Pasta Salad 52
    Thick and Hearty Clam Chowder 52
Shrimp-and-Pasta Salad 52
Side dishes. *See also*
    Breads; *Desserts*; *Dips*; *Salads*
    Asparagus with Egg Sauce 59
    Creamy Au Gratin Potatoes 57
    Festive Rice 55
    Gourmet Mashed Potatoes 56
    Green Beans with Almonds 58
    Mashed Potatoes Florentine 56
    Rice Pilaf 55
    Stewed Apples 61
Soup
    Cream of Tomato Soup 53
    Thick and Hearty Clam Chowder 52
South of the Border Pork Tenderloin 46
Spaghetti Sauce with Meat 40
Spicy Skillet Pork 45
Steak and Cheese Braid 42
Stewed Apples 61
Stir-Fry 45
    Beef Vegetable Stir-Fry 41
    Hawaiian Sausage Stir-Fry 45

T

Tangy Vegetable Potato Salad 57
Thick and Hearty Clam Chowder 52
Tomato and Avocado Salad 59

V

Vegetarian Chimichangas 50
Vegetarian main dishes
    Cheese Ravioli with Marinara 50
    Cream of Tomato Soup 53
    Vegetarian Chimichangas 50

W

Waldorf Salad 60

*"How wonderful it is, how pleasant,
for God's people to live together in harmony!"*
—PSALM 133:1 (TEV)

Order Form

Please send the following books published by Purrfect Publishing Ltd.

Title	Quantity	Price (see back cover)	Total
Homemade To Go	____ x	$14.95	$ ____
_____	____ x	_____	$ ____
_____	____ x	_____	$ ____

Subtotal = $ ____

Shipping

Book Rate: $2.00 for the first book and 75 cents for each additional book (allow three to four weeks)
Priority: $3.50 per book

5% tax (ID residents) = $ ____
Shipping (at left) = $ ____
Total = $ ____

Name: _____
Address: _____
City: _____ State: _____ Zip: _____ - ____
Telephone: (____) ____ - _____

Mail this form and check (or money order) to:
Purrfect Publishing - Dept. B, P.O. Box 1013, Meridian, ID 83680-1013.

Questions? Comments? Recipe ideas? Write to the address above or e-mail us at CoCooking@aol.com.

Order Form

Please send the following books published by Purrfect Publishing Ltd.

Title	Quantity	Price (see back cover)	Total
Homemade To Go	____ x	$14.95	$ ____
_____	____ x	_____	$ ____
_____	____ x	_____	$ ____

Subtotal = $ ____

Shipping

Book Rate: $2.00 for the first book and 75 cents for each additional book (allow three to four weeks)
Priority: $3.50 per book

5% tax (ID residents) = $ ____
Shipping (at left) = $ ____
Total = $ ____

Name: _____
Address: _____
City: _____ State: _____ Zip: _____ - ____
Telephone: (____) ____ - _____

Mail this form and check (or money order) to:
Purrfect Publishing - Dept. B, P.O. Box 1013, Meridian, ID 83680-1013.

Questions? Comments? Recipe ideas? Write to the address above or e-mail us at CoCooking@aol.com.